Anyone can tell a STORY

Bob Hartman's Guide to Storytelling

A Lion Children's Book
an imprint of
Lion Hudson plc
Mayfield House, 256 Banbury Road,
Oxford OX2 7DH, England
www.lionhudson.com
ISBN 0 7459 4587 2

First edition 2002
10 9 8 7 6 5 4 3 2

A catalogue record for this book is available
from the British Library

Typeset in 10/13 Latin 725 BT
Printed and bound in Great Britain
by Cox and Wyman Ltd, Reading

Contents

Introduction

Four words. That's all it takes. And bodies lean forward, heads jerk to attention, eyes focus, and off you go!

Maybe the destination is outer space. Maybe it's some fantasy world. A jungle, perhaps. A castle. A desert. A cave. Or maybe it's just next door.

'Once upon a time' can take you anywhere! That's the wonder of storytelling. And, if you like to hear stories or make up stories, and particularly if you would like to tell stories, then I would like to share some of my ideas with you.

It will be a rather personal view of storytelling. Every storyteller is different, so all I can do is speak from my own experience. But I believe that by showing you how I wandered into storytelling, I might be able to help you find the confidence to wander into it as well. And 'wander' is most definitely the right word. A discovery here, a mistake there. Trials and errors. Successes and failures. That's how I learned to tell stories. It's how most people do it, I think. And, because that will inevitably be a part of your journey as a storyteller, too, it might be helpful to see what happened to someone else along the way.

After that things will get a little philosophical. Not heavy – I promise! – but we will try to get to the heart of telling a story. That's because I believe that it's hard to do something well (to grasp the 'how' of it) without first understanding why it works. And I think the 'why' may surprise you!

Next, we'll have a look at the structure of the stories. Like me, some of you may enjoy writing stories, and this section should be a great help to you. But even if you only want to retell someone else's story, knowing how a story works – tearing it apart and putting it back together again – can give you the kind of insight into that story that will make the telling fresh and unique.

Only then will we look at some practical tips and techniques for good storytelling. It may seem that we're taking the long way around. But trust me – having covered the earlier terrain, this part will make a lot more sense!

And, finally, because retelling Bible stories is a particular love of mine, we will conclude by taking a close look at that particular type of storytelling.

Will there be stories along the way, as well? Of course! Some of them are retellings, some are originals, and most of them have found their way into one of my other books (which you might like to have a closer look at, too!). They are cross-referenced here and there throughout the text to illustrate different points and principles (look for the 'Leap to page...' boxes), but you will find them collected together at the end of the book, because it was just plain easier to do it that way.

So are you ready? Heads up? Bodies forward? Eyes focused? Then let's go: 'Once upon a time, there was someone with a bright red book in her hands who wanted to learn to tell stories...'

Bob Hartman

Storytelling

1

A Storyteller's Story

I can't remember exactly when it started.

Was it that time under the blankets, late into the night, with the dimming torch and the second-hand copy of *The Call of the Wild*?

Was it the junior boys' Sunday school class and my grandma's grizzly account of Ehud's left-handed execution of evil King Eglon?

Or was it those prizes I won on the last day of school, the year I turned eight? The plastic dinosaur that I lost before the summer ended, and the book about the magic umbrella that my mother still reads to her grandchildren?

I can't remember exactly when it started. It just seems that I have always loved stories. And I suppose that is why I became a storyteller. It's the essential requirement, surely! But *how* I became a storyteller is another question entirely. And the place I'd like to start.

You see, I can't really claim to be an expert in the field of storytelling – not in the sense that I've read all the texts and manuals, attended all the seminars, and know all there is to know about the subject.

All I can really say is that I love stories, I tell stories, and when I do, people of all ages lean forward and listen and seem to love those stories, too. So what I *can* share are the tips and techniques and, particularly, the attitudes and approaches I have picked up along the way. I can tell you what has worked and what has failed, where I find stories, and how I

> 'Try, fail and start again.'

tear them apart and put them back together again as I prepare to tell them. Every storyteller is different, with his or her own personality – which is as influential on the storytelling as the story itself. So if you find something that's helpful along the way – brilliant! And if something else just won't work for you – then that's all right, too. Because that's how I learned to tell stories. By watching and listening, trying and failing, and starting all over again!

Here's how it all began…

Kids' Play

When I was twelve, my younger brother, Tim, came home one afternoon, desperate to do something in the school talent show. He found a Muppet pattern in a women's magazine (*Sesame Street* was something new, then!), and stitched together a few puppets on my grandmother's old sewing machine. All he needed was a script. So I wrote one for him. I can't honestly remember what it was about, but it began an eight-year run of puppet shows in schools, churches and at community festivals in the Pittsburgh area.

My other brother, Daryl, joined in as well – along with a few other friends. And my mum ferried us around in her beaten-up old Studebaker. We were just kids, but that experience taught us a lot about storytelling.

We discovered first of all how important it is to have interesting characters. Tim is a natural comedian and very quick-witted, so it didn't take us long to start building the stories around his puppets. We countered his cheeky irreverence with a collection of 'straight-man' type characters – typical stand-up fare – which helped us learn the place of conflict in storytelling, too. Bit by bit, we discovered the ways that characters can work together to create both humour and tension, and build the story to a satisfying conclusion.

We also learned how important it is to build a relationship with an audience. Puppeteers can only tell how their audiences are reacting through what they hear. We discovered, very quickly, how helpful it is to see those reactions as well. So we started putting someone 'out front' at the side of the stage, to be our eyes. He would sometimes act as a narrator, sometimes as a straight man, sometimes even as one of the characters. But, best of all, he would watch the crowd, gauge their reactions, and move things on or slow things down, depending on what he saw.

'Build a relationship with the audience.'

'Gauge the crowd's reactions.'

'Adapt and adjust.'

We learned a lot about story pacing and story length, as well. Our early stories were short and punchy, largely because we were pretty insecure, and wanted to get in there and get out as quickly as possible! But as our confidence grew, so did the stories. And that was a mistake. It was the era of the Rock Opera, and I suppose I fancied myself in that light – writing huge puppet extravaganzas. But they just didn't work. They meandered on and on, losing their point and their tension, and, worst of all, the audience! To this day, I would still rather do several short stories than one long one – because it gives me the chance to adapt and adjust (or simply bail out!) instead of being stuck in the middle of some epic.

Yes, we made mistakes – loads of them! Inadequate practice. Incomprehensible messages (when more than one parent or teacher wanted to know what 'that story was about'). And inappropriate humour (although I can still wet myself over most things scatological!). But the most important thing was that we learned from those mistakes and we improved, year by year.

There's one thing I can't emphasize enough – the only way you learn to tell stories and improve your storytelling abilities is to do it. Because I'm an author, people often ask me, 'How do I get a book published?' My usual response is, 'What have you written?' And you would be amazed at how many of them haven't written anything at all! Why? Sometimes it's fear, and sometimes it's uncertainty, and sometimes it's a lack of confidence. I can empathize – I have had those feelings myself. But unless you actually put those things behind you and have a go, you'll never write a book. The same thing is true of storytelling. You have to try, accepting from the start that you'll make mistakes, face difficult audiences, forget where you're going, and not always get it right. But you have to start somewhere. You have to take that leap. Maybe it's because we were just kids and didn't know any better – but we had a go. And, because we had a go, we learned a lot about telling stories.

'Learn from your mistakes.'

'Start somewhere – have a go!'

University Challenge

I learned a lot about stories at university, too. I was studying theology, preparing for a career as a church minister, and was surprised to discover that this helped me to understand even

13

more about the way that stories work, and the power they have to affect us.

The Bible – the basic text of all theological students – is essentially a collection of stories. It contains other genres, I know, but the bulk of the Bible relates events in the history of Israel and then the life of Jesus as stories – stories that are meant to help us understand both who God is and who we are. Preaching, therefore, has much to do with storytelling. Yes, I tried some of the other approaches – three points and a conclusion, unpacking the apostle Paul's tightly knit theological arguments, wrestling with the vivid imagery in the psalms. But what I discovered very early in my preaching career was that people responded best to stories. They leaned forward, they listened, they laughed, they cried – they got the point! So I just kept on telling stories.

That was a challenge, at first, because the people in my church had already heard many of those stories, and there's nothing worse than that 'Oh, here's THAT story again' look. As any parent knows, you can tell the same story to a small child time and time again. But it's different with older children and adults. A familiar story is a lot like a joke when you've already heard the punchline. You know how it's going to end, so you don't pay as much attention. I worked hard to find a way around that problem. So if I was retelling a well-known Bible story, I tried my best to find a unique 'way in' to the story. Sometimes I told it from a different perspective – from the 'bad guy's' point of view, perhaps! Sometimes I introduced a character who could be an objective observer of all that went on. Sometimes I started the story at an unfamiliar place. Anything to keep the listeners guessing, so that when they finally realized which story it was, they were interested enough to listen until the

'Find a "way in" to a story.'

end. There's nothing original about this of course – the spate of reworked and re-imagined fairy tales that have appeared over the last few years attests to the fact that this works with other kinds of stories as well. And that's the important thing about a fresh approach – it re-establishes the kind of tension and expectancy that pulls an audience through a story.

The other thing that preaching taught me was the way that an audience relates to the characters in a story. Many people who aren't familiar with the Bible assume that it's a pious, holier-than-thou kind of book. The fact of the matter is that the Bible is brutally honest about the people whose lives it chronicles, and we see them – even the 'heroes' – warts and all. That means that people can identify with the characters in a Bible story, both at their best times and at their worst. And, because the stories are human and honest, they encourage people to be honest about themselves.

One Sunday, I told the story of the prodigal son (a moving tale about a father's love and forgiveness for his wayward child) and was surprised when one of the older ladies in the church told me which character she related to. It wasn't the son who'd run away and wanted his father to accept him back. And it wasn't the father who longed for his son to return.

Leap to page 70

No, it was the older brother who had never left home who resented the attention that the wayward son received on his homecoming. It was a moment of honesty – about her own life, and her struggle to come to terms with the negative feelings she had for her own brothers and sisters who had left her to care for an elderly parent. That wasn't really the point of my message, but it was what she came away with. And it gave me an opportunity to talk about the ways that the mercy shown by the father might make a difference in her life, as well.

Developing My Own Style

My first church was in Wigston, a suburb of Leicester. My children were both born there, and when that work came to an end, we moved back to Pittsburgh, primarily so that my wife and I could raise the kids near their extended family. My brother Tim was working in children's theatre at the time, but was interested in developing his career in a new direction. He had done some storytelling at one of the big Pittsburgh libraries and thought that by telling stories together, he and I could recreate the same dynamic that had worked so well with the puppets, years before. So I took a break from the ministry and joined him.

We took one of the stories he had been telling – Pittsburgh's tall tale about a heroic steel worker called Joe Magarac – and adapted it to our own style. What we came up with was a kind of 'tag team' approach to storytelling. Sometimes we would alternate telling the narrative bits. Sometimes we would cross over into drama, with each of us taking different 'parts'. And sometimes it would look more like a stand-up comedy routine, as we borrowed the 'straight man'/'funny man' stuff from our puppeteering days.

Leap to page 72

I suppose the purist would argue that it wasn't straightforward storytelling. And it wasn't. It was a fusion of a lot of different styles and approaches. But the bottom line was that it worked! Kids loved it. Teachers did, too. And I continued to learn more about telling stories.

Structure and Control

First of all, I learned about the importance of structure, control and rules in a storytelling context. This was essential for our work in school assemblies. In the USA, these usually last for

45–50 minutes, and are either made up of the whole school together, or the school broken into two big groups (corresponding roughly to infants and juniors in the UK). So the average session was two to three hundred children, although I can recall times when that number jumped to five or six hundred! In addition, we were usually working in rooms that were not the best, acoustically – barn-sized gymnasiums where the sound echoed everywhere or ancient auditoriums with squeaky folding seats. In that kind of situation, we found that we needed some way to keep the children as quiet as possible (or to re-establish that quiet following some noisy participation activity that we had instigated!).

In his children's theatre work, Tim had come across a device that many teachers use – and we found that it worked for us, as well. He started each programme by telling the children that they were going to have a great time. They would see things that they liked, and maybe even things that they didn't like. But most of all, they would see things that made them laugh, and perhaps make them want to say something to their neighbour. He assured them that we understood that, but also pointed out that too much whispering would make it hard to hear the story. Then Tim would stick his arm straight up in the air. (He's a tall guy and would sometimes smack his hand up against a low ceiling. The kids loved that!) 'When you see my hand go up,' Tim would say, 'then everyone needs to be quiet as quickly as possible and look straight up here.'

'Think about structure, control and rules.'

'Keep storytelling devices simple.'

And that was it. It seems simple, I know. Almost too simple to work! But it did. And I think it did, precisely because it was simple.

The device was just a way of giving us the room to work and the opportunity to be heard in the first place. With rowdier groups, we had to reinforce it more at the start – so that they would get the idea, and understand that we really meant it. And, yes, there was the odd occasion when we did have to give in and simply carry on in spite of the noise. But 97% of the time, it worked. (I've tried hard to forget about the other 3%!) And the kids really enjoyed themselves.

Respect

During this time, I also learned a lot about respecting children. Tim and I often had the chance to listen to other storytellers, and some of them felt the need to adopt a sickly-sweet tone of voice when talking to children. We were determined, from the start, to talk to children in our natural voices – to try to be ourselves when we were with them. I think that showed that we respected and valued them. And it was probably one of the reasons that we received their respect in return.

This approach also helped to engage teachers in our stories. Quite often, teachers would get the kids settled for the beginning of the assembly, and then would mark papers while the assembly was going on. Tim and I decided that one of our goals would be to get the teachers to put away their work and listen! Tossing in the odd adult reference or joke certainly helped, but so did the fact that we didn't talk down to the kids and made it clear that the stories we told were for 'everybody'.

> 'Don't talk down to children.'

Keeping it Simple

Finally, I think I learned a lot about simplicity. Many of the schools we visited had hosted assemblies that required elaborate lighting and sets. And with certain kinds of productions, that's necessary. But it isn't with storytelling. In fact, Tim and I agreed early on that we would take no more into an assembly than what the two of us could carry in one trip (or that would squeeze into the back of his Honda!). That meant the obligatory cup of coffee in one hand, and a stool, or a coat rack, or a plastic dustbin full of props in the other. We took turns sitting on the stool. We used a few props for each programme. And the coat rack? Well, as we enjoyed explaining to the kids during the question and answer session – that was for hanging our coats on! And it provided some kind of backdrop – a

'You don't need lots of fancy props, sets and lights.'

concession, I suppose, to the comments we would sometimes overhear – 'You mean we spent hundreds of dollars for this?!' The assumption, of course, was that a presentation without lots of fancy props and sets and lights couldn't possibly engage the children. But that assumption was wrong. Storytelling doesn't require anything but engaged imaginations. Not even coat racks and dustbins. And we proved that, time and time again.

Once a little girl – not more than seven or eight years old – came up to me after a session. And her comments say it all. 'That story you told,' she said, her eyes full of wonder, 'I could see it! I could see everything! The old man, the mountain, the waves. I could see it!' In an age when we bombard our children with visual and aural stimulation, it's a real thrill to hear

Leap to page 76

those words. Because, given half a chance, children's imaginations can run free – as they were meant to. And they can see! They really can. If only we're willing to keep things simple.

Tim and I toured for a year on our own, and then were spotted by some folks from the Pittsburgh Children's Museum at a performers' showcase. They asked us to become a part of their team representing them in schools, which we did for the next ten years. We carried on telling 'Joe Magarac', but then went on to create five more storytelling programmes. This took us to the magic number of six – 'magic' because six is the number of grades there are in the average American elementary school. And that means that you can go back to the same school, year after year, and never have to repeat a programme to the same audience!

Looking back on it, it's strange to think that all those stories (and quite a few more, actually) were bouncing around in our heads at one time – particularly since I'm not that great at memorizing. Maybe that will be an encouragement, if that's your situation, too. There's no better way to get really comfortable with a story, plumbing the depths of its power and effectiveness, than by telling it again and again and again. And I can say with confidence that we told some of those stories hundreds of times and more!

'Repetition brings confidence.'

At the same time, however, we were both involved in individual pursuits. I took up writing books for children, and Tim landed better and better acting jobs, both on stage and in film. (In *The Silence of the Lambs*, in the scene where Hannibal Lecter talks with the Senator, Tim is the secret agent with the moustache, standing in the background!) In the end, the time came when we each needed to give more attention to those other pursuits. So Tim carried on with his acting, and I moved to the UK, to promote my books, tell stories in schools, and teach others how to tell stories, too. Which brings us to the present, and the rest of this book!

Sources for Stories

The best thing a storyteller can do is to read lots and lots of stories!

• **Traditional.** There are fine collections of traditional folk tales available in libraries and bookshops. Try to read stories from a variety of cultures. You will find some familiar ones that appear right across the world (and make for interesting retellings because of the cultural differences) and some that you will never have heard before. Retell the ones you like. It's as simple as that. And if it's a traditional tale, don't be afraid to play around with it a bit. Change details if that fits your style or situation – tellers have been doing that for ages!

• **Contemporary.** I think it's also all right to retell contemporary stories that you find in modern picture books. It certainly doesn't matter to me if someone tells one of my stories to a crowd. Just be sure to give credit to the author (waving the book about and mentioning the title and ISBN is even more helpful!).

• **Some of my favourites.** Bible stories are a wonderful resource. I like starting with the Bible itself, but there are lots of good retellings available, as well. There are also some fine stories to be found in the lives of the saints, the history of the church, and (one of my personal favourites) the lives of the Desert Fathers.

2

How Stories Work

Mr McKee, my sixth grade teacher, was different from any teacher I'd ever had before. For a start, he was a man, unlike most primary school teachers at that time. And then there was that other thing – the thing that happened one Friday afternoon, early in the autumn term.

Mr McKee asked us to put away our books and pencils and papers. (Let's face it, when you're a kid, that request alone is enough to make you sit up and take notice!) Then he walked slowly round the room, pulling down the blinds, one by one. Finally, he turned off a few lights so that the room was dark and cool. Everyone looked around. We couldn't imagine what would happen next! And that's when Mr McKee went to the front of the room, reached behind his desk, pulled out a copy of *The Lion, the Witch, and the Wardrobe* and began to read.

As far as I can remember, that's how every Friday afternoon went, for the rest of that term. And we listened, rapt – many of us for the first time – to the adventures of Lucy and Edmund and Peter and Susan, as they wandered through the wardrobe and into the land of Narnia. It was my first exposure to those books and, along with many of my classmates, I rushed to the library afterwards to pick up a copy for myself. But more than that, it was the first time that

I ever felt what I now believe lies at the heart of every good storytelling experience. Intimacy. Community. Relationship.

Building Relationships

Relating to the Audience

Before the story itself, before any 'tips' and 'techniques', good storytelling is all about relationships. And the first and most important relationship is the one that develops between the storyteller and the audience.

To be honest, I have struggled with the term 'audience' for some time now, because it suggests a passive group of listeners who simply receive what is offered to them. But there is nothing passive about what happens in a good storytelling session. At the best of times, it is an occasion where the teller and the crowd build something together.

You see, storytelling is not about someone tossing out a mouthful of words for others to catch. It is about that thing that is created between them – the result of imagination and participation and eye contact and laughter and tears. Storytelling is not a presentation, it's a conversation. It's not a performance, it's a dialogue.

> 'Good storytelling is all about relationships.'

> 'Storytelling is a conversation, a dialogue.'

So the same story can be different every time you tell it – because the crowd is different, or the context is different, or the responses are different. During the course of a party, for example, you might say the same things to a number of different people. But the way you say them, the order and the emphasis will have a lot to do with the way those people respond to you. The same thing is true of storytelling. The crowd thinks that it is watching you, listening to you. The secret is that you are watching them, listening to them, and responding to them, as well!

When my brother and I started telling stories in school assemblies, someone would inevitably try to turn the 'house' lights off. I think the assumption was that the children would be quieter in the dark, as they would be in a theatre or a cinema. Well, if you've ever been in a dark cinema full of kids, you know that's not necessarily the case! But – even worse – Tim and I couldn't see the children! And seeing them – their responses, their reactions – was essential to building a relationship with them. I have the same problem when it comes to telling stories to very large groups of people – several thousands or so. I'm not saying it can't be done. It's just harder, because the feedback is limited primarily to what I can hear. There's so much more information when I can see, as well. And the more information, the better, because it's all about building that relationship – seeing people's reactions and hearing their response; shaping the story to suit that particular crowd. If the relationship works, the story will, too.

So how do you build a relationship with a group of people? I think you do it in the same way you would with an individual.

★ **Be yourself.** Resist the temptation to use a 'sickly sweet' voice with children or a 'pious' voice if you're telling Bible stories. Just be honest about who you are. If you're big and loud and noisy, then your storytelling will probably be pretty boisterous. But if you're quieter, let your stories reflect that – don't try to be something you're not.

★ **Be confident.** Even if you're shaking inside! Children, in particular, can smell the fear and the uncertainty. But even adult groups feel more comfortable when the person 'up front' seems relaxed.

★ **Be friendly.** Smile as you introduce yourself or set down the ground rules for the kids. Let them know right from the start that this is going to be a good experience, that everyone is going to have fun.

★ **Be fun!** Start with something funny – or at least something fun. Most people would rather laugh than cry, so save the serious stuff for later – for just the right moment. It will go down so much better when it comes as a surprise.

★ **Be smart.** Choose your first story carefully. If I'm doing a half-hour or forty-five minute session, I seldom tell only one long story. I do lots of little ones, because that gives me the chance to learn something about the group. I usually start with a story that I know really well, partly because of the 'confidence' thing, but more importantly because it gives me the freedom to watch and listen to the crowd and gauge their responses. Is there a particular kind of humour that they like? Are there a few listeners who are really getting into it? I'll keep my eye on them, and look for a little support if things get shaky later! And as for the ones who look as if they want to leave – I remind myself to try something different with them in the next story, because it takes longer for some people to warm to you than others (it's that relationship thing again!). But what if some people never warm to you? Well, stop looking at them and focus instead on the ones who are really enjoying your stuff!

Relating to the Characters

There is another relationship that is important to storytelling – the one that develops between those who hear the story and the characters in the story itself. Think of your favourite fairy tale. Which character do you like the best? With whom do you identify? One of my clearest childhood memories has to do with our picture book of 'The Three Little Pigs'. I can remember getting very upset every time the Big Bad Wolf fell down the chimney and landed in the boiling stewpot. I'm not sure what it says about me, but I liked the Big Bad Wolf! (Hey, he worked hard, he stuck to it, he was just doing what wolves do! And that brick-house pig always looked so smug!).

'Identify with the characters in your story.'

'Stories have the power to change values.'

It's this 'identification with characters' that makes any good narrative work. Think of your favourite film, your favourite soap opera, your favourite drama or situation comedy. The best ones are always character-driven, because it's the relationship that develops between you and those characters that keeps you watching. And it's true for storytelling, as well. It's like that moment when you turn over the last page of a good book and wish that you could spend just a little more time with those characters. If you have told the story well, then your audience will have identified with one character or another and maybe even experienced some sense of discovery or transformation along with that character. And that can be a very powerful experience, indeed.

I am convinced that storytelling has the power to shape and change lives. It really can lead to new discoveries – new ways of thinking and acting. And that brings us to the third relationship that is significant in storytelling – the relationship of storytelling to a particular community.

Relating to One Another

Traditionally, storytelling was the means by which values, histories and cultural expectations were passed from one generation to another. Whether the storyteller was a priest or a bard, the point of the story was not simply to entertain, but also to shape minds and to teach – to define what was good and bad, what was cowardly and heroic, what was acceptable and unacceptable. And, as those of you who are familiar with the parables of Jesus will know, stories could even be used to challenge deeply held cultural values and assumptions.

I always have a little chuckle when I hear film-makers argue that cinema has no direct effect on the way that people behave. Either they have no understanding of what they are doing, or they hope that we don't. Film and television are the chief means that our modern culture uses to access stories. And stories shape cultures. The proof lies in the enormous amount of money that corporations are willing to invest in all those little stories we call advertisements. Do you think for a minute that they would go on spending that kind of money if they weren't confident that those little stories had the power to change our buying habits? Storytelling is powerful precisely because it is subtle and subversive, because it can sneak up on you and surprise you. And that's why it needs to be used responsibly.

Challenging values by storytelling sometimes comes unexpectedly. Several years ago, my brother and I told a story about self-sacrifice to a class of eleven-year-olds in a Pittsburgh city school. It was a story we had told successfully on a number of occasions, about a rabbit who gives up his life for a field mouse. When the story was finished, the kids just stared at us for a minute, looks of shock and disbelief on their faces.

'Use storytelling responsibly.'

'That was stupid!' one of them said, at last. 'Why would that bunny die for a field mouse?'

'Yeah,' echoed several others in the class. 'It doesn't make any sense!'

We tried our best to explain that giving up something you wanted for the good of someone else could be worthwhile. But they just didn't 'get it'. Maybe it was the way we told the story. Maybe it was just that particular group of kids. But we came away from that experience determined to make sure that more of our audiences heard more of that kind of story – to provide some balance to the 'take-what-you-can-get-and-kill-as-many-people-along-the-way' material that finds its way into too many children's lives.

We quickly discovered that schools were really hungry for those kind of stories. Without sounding 'preachy', they provide a way of talking about all those 'citizenship' and 'values' issues that teachers sometimes struggle to communicate. So if you think there's too much violence, intolerance and hatred in your community, there's something you can do about it. You can tell stories – stories that are just as powerful, just as exciting, and just as much fun as all those violent tales, but stories that are about gentleness, forgiveness, peace and love.

Leap to page 79

Stories not only have the power to shape communities, but are also a means by which we can build a sense of community. A lot of communication these days requires only a face in front of a screen. But storytelling is all about a face in front of a face – faces together, in fact, sharing laughter and tears, surprise and joy. And today that's not a common experience for many children – or adults either, for that matter. True, it's more threatening in some ways than sitting alone in front of your television. You might laugh out loud at the wrong time, or have to wipe a tear from an eye. But it's ultimately more rewarding, for it's a chance to discover (or perhaps rediscover!) what happens when people experience a story together. It's what happens in churches, at the best of times. And in classrooms, too, when teachers can find some room in the straitjacket of the National Curriculum to sit down and relax with their class around a book.

This sharing is also happening in the storytelling groups that are springing up all around the country. And, I'm told, there are still places where it happens in pubs on a regular basis. But why not in hospitals and old folks' homes and corporate headquarters, as well? Why shouldn't storytelling have a place everywhere that people come together? For, as we draw parallels from the stories we hear with our own lives, we become closer to one another. We understand, we sympathize. And, hopefully, we experience a deeper sense of community.

> 'Storytelling can build a sense of community.'

Making the Conversation Work

Find a 'Way In'
If storytelling really is more a dialogue than a monologue, then someone has to get the conversation started. And that is why it is so important for the storyteller to decide how he or she is going to tell the story.

You mean you don't start with 'Once upon a time' and finish with 'And they all lived happily ever after'? Not necessarily. In fact, one of the great challenges of storytelling is finding a 'way in' to the story – that 'hook', device or gimmick, if you like, that pulls the listener in and makes the experience memorable. Some of the people in the group may have heard your story before. As I suggested earlier, this is particularly true of biblical storytelling, where preachers, Sunday school teachers and RE co-ordinators alike are faced with the annual task of finding an inventive 'way in' to the Christmas and Easter narratives (not to mention the stories of Noah, Jonah, and David and Goliath). The last thing you want is to encounter that groaning, been-there-done-that look. And even if the story you are telling is new to the audience, it is still better to tell that story as creatively as possible – so they hear the story at its best, the first time out.

So what do you do? You can start by just 'playing around' with the story. Several years ago, I was asked to write a book about angels. The subject was all the rage at the time, and I didn't want to write a book that was just like the rest. So I took a close look at the Bible stories about angels and asked a couple of questions. What if God created angels in the same way that he made us? Not white, winged clones, but unique individuals, suited to particular tasks. What if an angel's appearance was linked to the job it was called to do? I tried to answer those questions in the book, and that is why, in *Angels, Angels All Around*, the angel who is sent to make a meal for Elijah in the desert bears a striking resemblance to a TV chef. The angel who leads Peter out of prison is a clever little Puck of a fellow. And the angel who rescues Daniel from the lions' den looks a bit like a lion himself and plays through the night with the beasts so their attention is diverted from their dinner! Was I reading between the lines? Certainly. But I believe that asking questions of the story is one means of finding a unique way into it.

Leap to page 81

Another 'way in' is to alter the point of view from which the story is told. In my book, *Bible Baddies*, for example, I have retold familiar Bible stories from the point of view of the villains. The message of the story remains the same (and, in fact, sometimes becomes even clearer!), but the fresh approach really grabs an audience's attention. This works really well with other kinds of stories, too. You may be familiar with best-selling American writer John Sciezka, who has given us the

Leap to page 84

story of the Three Little Pigs from the wolf's point of view. But why not Red Riding Hood from the same angle, the Troll's take on the Billy Goats Gruff, or the Hare's view of his race with the Tortoise? The possibilities are endless. Starting from an unfamiliar place can make a well-known story really riveting, because the listeners are always wondering whether the ending will be same as before, and, if so, how you'll get there. And more than anything else, it's just good fun!

The trick is to surprise and to delight your listeners, because that is when they are truly open to the power of the story itself. As Aesop suggested in his fable about the sun and the wind, whimsy, humour, joy and delight are more effective paths to discovering truth and experiencing change than any heavy-handed approach. Granted, some stories are just for fun. But you will also be called upon to tell stories that are, by their very nature, more serious. Whatever the case, finding an original 'way in' to the story, and surprising your audience, will open that story up – even to those who have heard it a hundred times before.

By now, I hope I have made it clear that thinking about a story – what it means, the

'Find a device that pulls in your listeners.'

'Ask questions of the story to get a fresh approach.'

'The possibilities are endless.'

'ways in', how it works – is just as important as any technique you might use to tell it. It's the first step, really. And one that often gets overlooked. So, how do stories 'work'?

Find the Problem

For a start, every story should have one central problem. And it is the problem that drives the story – that makes the listener stay with the story to the end, to discover how that problem is resolved. Will Cinderella get to the ball? Will Red Riding Hood escape the Wolf? Will the Tortoise win the race, or will the Hare? Those are the problems that push these stories along. So the problem needs to be stated early and then used to build the tension throughout the story.

With some stories, there is more than one central problem to choose from. You might be familiar with the Bible story about Zacchaeus (an unpopular tax collector who changes his ways after Jesus dines with him). But is this a story about a bad man who needs forgiveness, a lonely man who needs acceptance, a short man who can't see, or a town that needs to understand Jesus' priorities regarding the company he keeps? The main problem could be any of these, but it can't really be all of them – not in one story, anyway. You have to choose which problem you want to drive the story right from the start, because the way you tell the story (the point of view you choose, the participation exercises you use – everything, in fact) will depend upon the problem you want to resolve.

Leap to page 89

It's also not uncommon for stories to have too many problems to solve in one sitting. The Bible story of Joseph, extremely familiar now because of his 'Technicolor Dreamcoat', is a good example of that. The story comes to us in several episodes: Joseph the dreamer, Joseph the slave,

Joseph the servant of Potiphar, Joseph the prisoner, Joseph the ruler, and Joseph the saviour of his people. Each of those episodes has its own driving problem. So it might be best to tell it in several sittings, or at least as several episodes.

Choose your problem – that's the key thing. For it will affect everything else you do.

Choose the Characters

Next, who are the main characters? Think about them, as well. In the course of a 5–10 minute story, you won't have time for a cast of thousands (unless, of course, you want some group participation!). What do your main characters want? In other words, how do they relate to the problem? And who are they? I'm not necessarily talking about in-depth character analysis, here. It's not as if you're De Niro preparing for your next film! But it is helpful to know the main characters well enough so that you can find just the right voice, or posture, or facial expression to make them come alive. I try to find two or three adjectives to describe each character – and that's usually enough.

Select the Setting

What is the setting of the story? That's the question you have to ask next. Many stories are utterly dependent on the audience knowing what the setting is. Imagine the Three Little Pigs without their houses, the Troll without his bridge, or Cinderella without a fancy ballroom. All right, you've got the freedom to change and update those settings if you like. And that can be great fun! But your audience will still need to

'The problem drives the story.'

'Know your characters well.'

'Keep descriptions simple.'

know where they are! There's no need for a lengthy, flowery description. That may have worked, once upon a time, but these days I think it can unnecessarily slow down the pace of the story. It's the problem that drives the story – remember – and a lot of descriptive language can clog up the traffic! So, as with your characters, keep the descriptions simple and clear. Trust me (or if not me – then all the editors I've ever worked with!), a few well-chosen words can be more accurate and poetic than a paragraph's-worth of bad ones.

You can sometimes even give your audience the chance to 'be' the setting. This won't work with every story, obviously, but it can be very effective with some. When I tell the Bible story about Jesus calming the storm, I ask the audience to rock gently back and forth. They become the waves on the sea. They become the setting. And not only do they hear about Jesus' power to still storms, but they experience it as well!

Leap to page 91

Find the Right Pace

Finally, there is the matter of pacing – finding your way from beginning to middle to end. My rule of thumb is to get the problem established as quickly as possible. And unless the audience knows what the problem is, and understands it clearly – then you're just coasting!

Next, take some time in the middle to build the tension towards a resolution. Traditional stories make use of the 'group of three' rule, here. The Troll meets not one, not two, but three Billy Goats Gruff before he is defeated. The Big Bad Wolf blows down two houses and tries his best to knock down a third before he ends up in the chimney. Other stories can work in this way, as well. I'm not suggesting that you artificially create three events in the middle of a story, if that's not appropriate to that particular tale. It's the proportions that are important to remember. If there is too much going on (the Big Bad Wolf moves from the house of straw, to the house of sticks, to the house of bricks, to the house of aluminium siding, to the house of concrete blocks, and so forth!) your audience will get bored. But if there is too little going on (the Big Bad Wolf blows down the first house and eats all the pigs) then there is no tension at all – and no story either, just an unfortunate incident! To borrow a phrase from Goldilocks, a little girl who also had to deal with groups of three, the middle of the story has to be 'just right!'

And, finally, the end! Quite simply, it has to be punchy and precise. If there is some phrase that you have repeated throughout, you might want to finish with it. Or perhaps some action you have asked your audience to do. What you want to avoid is just trailing off, like the 'fade' at the end of a pop song. Resolve your problem – make a big deal of it – and then tie it up nice and neat. There is nothing more satisfying than a good ending. So I will often try to decide, quite early on in my preparation of a story, how I will go about finishing it. There's nothing more wonderful than the 'ooh' or the 'aww' or the 'wow' or just the stunned silence you get from an audience when an ending has worked well.

'Maintain the pace and the tension.'

'Decide early on how you're going to finish the story.'

3

Tips and Techniques

When I was a boy, I had lots of little plastic dinosaurs and farm animals and toy soldiers and cars and trucks. On the days that we couldn't go outside, my two brothers and I would take all of those little plastic toys, dump them into a pile on the middle of the floor, and spend ages choosing which ones we wanted on our 'team'. Then, when all the choosing was done, we'd act out little adventures with those toys. We'd visit each other's 'houses', and drive around in the cars, and at some point a battle would inevitably break out, and somebody's toys would go flying down the stairs!

What were we doing? We were playing. And when it comes down to it, I believe that's what storytelling is all about. It's play – a verbal kind of play. So whenever I prepare to stand before a crowd, the first thing I do is to try to get myself into the right frame of mind and 'go' to what I call the place of play.

The Place of Play

I'm not sure where the place of play is exactly. It's in my head, and in my memories, and in my heart, all at once. But I know when I'm there. And I think that the children I share the stories with know that, too. It's as if they can see it in my eyes, sense it in my voice, pick up on it as we build that all-important relationship. It's a place they're familiar with, you see. And also a place where adults seldom go. So when they sense an adult *is* in the place of play, they lean forward, they listen, they smile. And they want to see what is going to happen next! They are surprised and delighted all at once. That's because, for just a short while, we enter their world – with their rules and expectations, instead of forcing them into our world.

'Go to the place of play.'

Frankly, I think the same thing applies to storytelling with adults. One of the reasons adults enjoy it is because they get to 'play', to be children again, for a while, to go to some never-never land, some once-upon-a-time place, and be in touch with the best kinds of childhood memories. I know that's true, not only because of what I see in the expressions of the adults who enjoy a good story, but also because of what I have seen in the eyes of those who try their hardest to resist it. I've told lots of stories in churches over the years, and there are always a few adults who really struggle with that experience. For some reason – maybe because their own childhood wasn't a happy time – they just don't want to 'go' to that place of play. And they know that's where a story will take them.

Being in the place of play simply makes it easier to be a good storyteller. When I'm in the place of play, I'm relaxed, I'm looking forward to what will happen next, it's easier to respond to the unexpected, and I'm in the mood to have fun (which is even possible with quite serious stories). When I'm not in the place of play – when I'm tired, maybe, or just not happy to be in front of a crowd on that day – I can feel the difference, I really can. I'm tense, I'm more nervous, I'm less likely to pick up on those little things that happen in the audience that help to make the stories come alive. It's simply harder to build that all-important relationship. I don't see or hear the audience as well. I get frustrated more easily if things go wrong. It's a bit like sport, I guess. When a football player or a tennis player is relaxed and into the game, then there's a flow, an energy to what they do that can turn even the biggest mistake into something good. For a storyteller – that 'zone' is the place of play.

The Place of Commitment

The place of play is also a place of commitment. When children play, they rarely do it half-heartedly. They throw themselves into it – doing whatever the scenario, the game, the situation demands. When I was a kid, I can't ever remember saying to my friends, 'Sorry, it's a bit embarrassing to have to pretend I'm a monster today.' Yes, we'd argue about who had to play what role – but that was always because there were some roles that were just plain better, usually because they were more, and not less, outrageous. Children can tell if you're in the place of play by your willingness to 'go for it' – to set aside the normal adult inhibitions and act in the joyful, unrestrained way that they do. And when you're in the place of play, you're more likely to want to behave like that yourself.

'Storytelling can set emotions free.'

'But what about the other adults in the room?' people often ask me. 'I'm all right when I'm on my own with the kids,' they say, 'but I don't want to look a fool in front of my friends or workmates or the other people in my church.' All I can suggest is this. Your willingness to go to the place of play and look like a fool will not only bring joy to the children in your audience (and get them on 'your side'), but will bring a little joy into the lives of your friends and colleagues as well! And what could be wrong with that? And I don't just mean that in a 'laugh at you and not with you' kind of way. The silliness, the goofiness, the joyful surprises or the honest tears that are a part of the best kind of storytelling – those simple and basic emotions are the very ones that can get suffocated as we become older and more sophisticated. Storytelling can set them free, and a part of us along with them.

There are some groups, however, who are not that keen on going to the place of play, and they make the hardest audiences. Adolescents, particularly, can be difficult, although I have even experienced this among younger children, especially in settings where groups from one or more schools have come together. There's a fear about not appearing 'cool' in front of their peers which often makes them very quiet and unresponsive. These groups require a slightly different approach.

It starts with remembering that 'relationship' thing again. Your goal is not to embarrass your audience (well, not till you know them, anyway!), so you do the best you can and start with a story that's pitched at their level and mood. If they're sitting back, arms folded, with that 'too cool for storytelling' look in their eyes, don't start with something that's too young, too silly, or requires too much participation. Give them something you're confident with, so that you can watch their reactions and find out what they like. Test the waters with a little participation. Will anyone volunteer? How do the others react? Try several different kinds of humour as well. Do they laugh the hardest at slap-stick, wordplay, or sarcasm? Find out what works and go with that. If, for some reason, you're committed to a serious story, then give it everything you've got and show you're treating them like the adults they consider themselves to be. Whatever you do, keep watching them. Get your energy from those who are responding positively. Ignore, for a while, at least, those who insist on training their eyes on the ceiling. They will come along, as more of the others do. You can count on it. And by the end of the session (this is my experience, anyway), they'll be 'playing' along with the rest of the audience – although they'd be horrified if you called it that!

Bringing Characters to Life

A Tried and Tested Tale

One of my all-time favourite stories is 'Aunt Mabel's Table'. It's one of the first ones I ever wrote and I've told it hundreds and hundreds of times. So many times, in fact, that when the marketing and sales people at my publishing house accompany me to promotional events, they run screaming from the room at the first words of the introduction! Every storyteller has a few stories like 'Aunt Mabel's Table' – stories that work so well, and they enjoy telling so much, that they can hardly keep themselves from doing it!

Leap to page 93

'Aunt Mabel' works for a couple of reasons, I think. It has an interesting problem (that's what drives the story – remember?). Five dinner guests. Five cans of food. You have to eat whatever is in the can you choose. But none of the cans has a label. It's like a culinary version of Russian roulette!

But what really makes the story work is the variety of characters around the table. There is Aunt Mabel, for a start, who has invented this little 'game'. At one point in the story, she is described as being 'different from other people'. There is her husband, Uncle Joe, who has allergic reactions to just about everything. There are her children, Sue (who is probably the most normal of the lot) and Tom, who got dog food the last time they played the game! And then there is Alexander – the visiting nephew – from whose point of view the story is told. These characters are talking constantly – guessing what is in each can and commenting on the contents. And so it's important that the audience can easily distinguish one from the other. That's the challenge of bringing a character to life.

> 'Make a clear distinction between your characters.'

When I first told this story, I took a hard at look at each of the characters, and as I suggested in the previous chapter, I found a couple of adjectives to describe each one. Then I tried to find a voice, a set of expressions, and a posture to 'portray' each character.

The Characters

• Aunt Mabel stands up straight and tall, her hands folded in front of her. Her voice is high and posh, with just a hint of barely disguised eccentricity! She smiles almost all the time – because she loves her strange little game.

• Uncle Joe, on the other hand, hates the game. He's stooped over. He's grumpy. And he's loud!

• Cousin Sue doesn't like the game either. But she knows it's not going away, so her voice suggests a sense of sad resignation.

• Cousin Tom is a bit of a geek. He's got a nasal voice and a buck-toothed expression that I use to convey his hope that he won't end up with yet another can of dog food.

• And Alexander? He's confused and nervous and just a little frightened by this curious dining experience. So I make his voice and actions small and tentative.

The idea is to make the characters interesting, funny and distinct. And to do it as simply as possible so that the change from one character to another doesn't interrupt the smooth flow of the story. That's why I have a problem with using lots of props and costumes. If I'm telling the story on my own, then the time that it takes to change hats or wigs or shirts usually distracts the audience from the story itself. The trick is to keep it simple – to find just the right 'face' or just the right 'posture' so that the character can be recognized immediately. Try them out in front of a mirror. That's one of the easiest ways to see if your expressions or postures work. If they make you laugh, then they will probably make your audience laugh as well. When my brother Tim was a kid, he used to spend hours in the bathroom. We thought he had digestive problems, but it turns out that he was just practising his silly faces! I'm sure that's one of the reasons he's so good at doing them now. And you will find better faces, too, if you try them out and work at them (and are part of a family with really strong bladders!). So think about your characters, try out a few faces and postures, and keep the characterization clear but simple.

'Practise facial expressions in front of the mirror.'

Voices

And that brings us to character voices. Lots of aspiring storytellers have told me that they struggle with creating voices, but I'm convinced that most people can do voices – five, at the very least!

For a start, most people can do some kind of 'high and squeaky' voice – a voice that would suit a little child or a fairy or a baby bird type character. I find that this voice works particularly well if you're a big guy. Kids love the humour that comes from that kind of contrast. So have a go. Why not try it out, right now! Take the first couple of lines of 'Twinkle twinkle little star' and do them in the highest and squeakiest and funniest voice you can do. If you do, you'll notice that that little voice is echoing around somewhere at the top of your throat, right smack in the middle.

Now move that same voice to the back of your throat and you'll be ready for the next one – the high, scratchy voice. This voice is great for squirrels and rabbits and hedgehogs and the like. It's cheekier than the pure high voice and works well with really mischievous characters. So go on. Try the 'Twinkle twinkle' thing again with that voice. It's at the top and the back of your throat.

Now go right to the bottom of your throat, but back in that echoey middle part again. That's where you'll find the big deep boomy voice. It's great for kings and giants. That's right – go on and try it. 'Twinkle twinkle' would be all right again – but you might want to use 'Fee-fi-fo-fum' this time to get just the right idea!

Now take the deep voice and go the back of your throat again, and that's where you'll find the rough growly voice.

Six Useful Voices

- High and squeaky
- High and scratchy
- Deep and boomy
- Rough and growly
- Nasal
- Don't forget your own!

43

This one works for angry giants or lions or tigers or anything really that's meant to be big and scary. A little warning, though – this one will make you want to clear your throat afterwards, and even cough sometimes – and so might interrupt the flow of the story. Someone also told me once that this voice is not particularly good for your throat and could cause damage if used too much. So use it sparingly. That will make it even more effective! So go on and try it, just to see how it works for you.

Finally, there is the nasal voice. Practise it by pinching your nose, just below the bridge, and speaking. This voice is great for those geeky characters, and you'll find that it won't be long before you can do it without the 'pinching' bit.

Leap to page 97

So you see, there are five voices that anyone can do. And when you add your own voice – there are six! The fact of the matter is that you probably won't need any more than that in the average story.

Accents

If you want to add some variation from story to story, you can always play around with whatever regional accents you can do. The UK is blessed with a wonderful variety of regional accents that can make for some very interesting characters and really bring stories to life.

But a couple of warnings here. First, you need to feel pretty confident about your accent before you use it. There's nothing better than when the audience recognizes and laughs along with a really good accent. And nothing worse than when the audience gives you that puzzled look that shows they can't figure out what it is you're trying to do! So it's probably best not to 'try out' an accent in the place from which that accent comes! Developing your Geordie accent in Swansea might go down just fine. But don't work on your Welsh one there!

It might also be best to avoid purely ethnic accents. There's a fine line here, I know. And it changes from culture to culture. But, as a white westerner, I would feel uncomfortable doing an Asian, Middle-eastern, or 'black' voice. It's too easy to stereotype. And, yes, I know that you could say the same thing about regional accents – but there doesn't seem to be the same risk of offence with those. And for some reason that I can't quite get my head around, everyone seems to laugh at a bad French accent. (Except, presumably, the French! Who knows? Maybe they get their laughs from bad English accents!) Anyway, try to be sensitive. The bottom line is that it's tough to build a good storytelling relationship with an audience you've already offended.

As with faces and postures, it's important that you find a voice that's appropriate to your character. Sometimes it can be fun to work against type. A giant with a little squeaky voice can be funnier than one with a big loud voice, for example. What you don't want to do, though, is to work against the problem in your story. If the giant is meant to be evil, it's probably best not to make him funny (unless you're going for a camp kind of evil). Or, if you have a character who is meant to have something quite sombre to say in the story, it might be better not to give him or her a silly voice. All you will get then are laughs when you are trying to be serious. This can be a particular problem in biblical storytelling when it comes to choosing a voice for God or for Jesus. I always go for some variation of my 'normal' voice for Jesus, and I work hard to erase any trace of that breathless, pious, religiousy tone (particularly since Jesus spent a lot of his time fighting against that very thing!). As far as the voice of God goes, the temptation is always to turn up the reverb and do the deep and boomy voice. I think that works sometimes, but it's also helpful to remember that, as in the Old Testament story of the prophet Elijah, God sometimes speaks in a 'still, small voice' as well!

Repetition

Here's a little quiz! When you think of the story of the Three Little Pigs, what phrase comes to mind? 'I'll huff and I'll puff and I'll blow your house down'? Or maybe 'Little Pig, Little Pig, let me in' and 'Not by the hair of my chinny-chin-chin'. And how about the phrase that you connect with the Three Bears? 'Who's been sleeping in my bed?', right? And Jack and the Beanstalk? 'Fee-Fi-Fo-Fum, I smell the blood of an Englishman!', of course!

And why do you remember those phrases? It's because they are repeated over and over again throughout those famous stories. Repetition is a very important part of traditional storytelling. And it's important for several good reasons.

First of all, repetition helps the storyteller to remember the story! Once upon a time, stories were not written down. They were passed on orally, from teller to teller. Repetitive devices helped to keep the story anchored in the teller's head. That's why repetition often takes place at the transition points in stories – to conclude one section or set up another. It saves the teller from having to think about how to get into the next part. It's there, in the head, as a kind of breathing space.

Similarly, repetition helps to make the story more memorable to the audience. Tim and I would go back to the same schools year after year, and invariably we would be greeted by kids shouting out a repetitive phrase from the year (and sometimes even four or five years) before. The phrases stuck – and so did the stories along with them.

Repetition also helps to build tension in a story. The audience soon catches on to the fact that certain phrases or

> ## Repetition
>
> - Helps the storyteller remember the story
> - Helps the listener remember the story
> - Helps build the tension
> - Helps encourage participation

actions will happen again and again. Then they look forward to the repetition, expect it, anticipate it, and enjoy it when it comes round again. So that if that repetitive device is linked to the problem in some way (as it often is), then it serves to create the kind of tension that every story needs on its way to a resolution.

Finally, repetition encourages participation. There is a wonderful Puerto Rican tale about a grandmother struggling to put her grandson to bed. The bedroom door is squeaky, and every time she shuts it, it wakes him up. So she fills his bed with a variety of pets to keep him company. The sounds of the door and the boy and the animals are repeated over and over again. And I find that I don't even have to tell the audience to make those sounds along with me. After I have repeated them once or twice, they catch on to how the story works and jump right in. That kind of spontaneous participation is a wonderful thing, but it only happens in that particular story because of the repetition.

Leap to page 100

Some of the stories that you tell will already have those repetitive devices built into them. I encourage you to use them. But if those devices are not there already, it's not that hard to come up with repetition of your own. Once again, keep it simple – a phrase, a response, an action (something that's easy to catch on to and fun to do) will keep your audience with you, right through to the end.

Participation

Now to what is, in my opinion, the most important storytelling device of them all. If storytelling is truly a dialogue, then someone needs to get the conversation started. If storytelling is really just a verbal form of play, then it's no fun to play alone. Participation is the ice-breaker that starts the conversation, the invitation for everyone to get down on their hands and knees and play.

Participation comes in many forms. At its simplest, a participation device is something that everyone in the group does together. Maybe it's an action that everyone does on cue. Maybe it's a line that everyone echoes back to the storyteller. Maybe it's a response that everyone makes when a certain word is spoken. Sometimes it's helpful to start the story by telling the crowd what they need to do at a certain point. (And sometimes it works just as well to ask them to do it when you get there.) The important thing, though, is that the participation device should be easy to catch on to (that simple thing again!), and fun to do.

'Participation is the most important device of all.'

A difficult participation activity is a bit like that part of the wedding where the bride and groom have to say their vows, and the vicar gives them those long wordy chunks to repeat. Everyone feels bad when the couple stumble and fumble and mispronounce the words. And the same thing can happen in a story.

48

But it can be just as bad when the participation activity simply isn't interesting. There's nothing better than being involved in a story where everyone is doing something together that's fun. And there's nothing worse than going through the motions to get through an activity that's not.

So how do you tell the difference? Well, you have your own experience to start with. Does a particular phrase, action, or response feel like it's fun to you? If not, then find something else. Certain things almost always work – silly noises (body noises particularly – but your repertoire really needs to extend beyond fitting raspberries somewhere into every story!), funny faces, and, for some reason, elephant and monkey impersonations. Exaggeration of any kind, in fact, will usually work – as long as you yourself are comfortable exaggerating, and having fun with it, too. That's the key, really. If you introduce an activity as if it's the best thing in the world, and the group sees that you're enjoying yourself, they are more likely to enjoy it, too. And more willing to have a go in the first place.

'Have fun, and your audience will have fun too.'

Participation activities where everyone is doing the same thing are probably the easiest kinds to initiate. There's more security for each individual if everyone looks foolish, and so you're likely to get more of the crowd involved. If some folks are not participating, however, don't harangue them. A little gentle encouragement is all right. Something like 'OK, everybody now!' But singling out non-participants will not win you many friends. Some are more shy than others. Some might be struggling to do the activity or to repeat the words – no matter how simple. Some might have certain disabilities, even, that make the activity more difficult for them. And some people just don't like to participate! So be gentle. Continue having fun with those who are joining in. And hope that those who aren't will catch the spirit of the thing and join in later. It's that relationship thing again. It will take longer for some folks to feel secure with you than for others. Give them time. And more often than not you will find them getting involved a story or two later.

Leap to page 103

Working with Little Children

A word or two about very small children, here. Many little children are frightened by loud noises. They can't stand them – they really can't. On the other hand, there are other small children who love to make loud noises! What do you do if that's one of your participation activities? You warn them, that's what. You say something like, 'We're going to make a really loud noise, and if you don't like loud noises, now is the time to hold your hands over your ears!' That won't spoil things for the kids who like to make the noises. In fact, it will give them time to take a really big breath! But it will prepare the kids who don't like them. And, surprisingly, it will give them the chance to make the noise, too – but in a safe and secure environment. I can't tell you how many little children I've seen – hands held tightly over their ears and shouting for all they're worth!

The next thing you want to keep in mind, when it comes to small children and participation, is what I call the 'Teletubby effect'. I learned this the hard way, actually. Up until a few years ago, I worked mainly with primary-school-aged children. But then my sister, who worked in a pre-school, asked me to tell some stories to her class. When the time came for participation, I did the kind of thing I normally did with older children – I asked three of the kids to come up front and play different parts. They were simple parts and the children did very well, but just as soon as the story had finished, the other children began to shout 'Again! Can we do it again?' You see, everybody wanted the chance to play those three parts! But in order to make that happen, I would have had to tell the story fifteen times at least! So now, when I tell stories to very small children, I give everybody the chance to do everything. And then we don't need to do it all over again! (Having said that, there is no reason that you can't repeat a story in a session, if the audience really wants you to. As a matter of fact, it happened just the other day during a story-building session with a brilliant class of Year

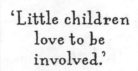

'Little children love to be involved.'

Sevens! It's the ultimate compliment, I suppose – that a group should enjoy a story so much that they want to repeat the experience.)

The final thing I need to say about participation and very small children is that they should not be put into situations where they feel too vulnerable or insecure. Once I was retelling the story of David and Goliath, and chose a four-year-old girl for the part of David. Unfortunately, I left David on her own for too long, while I dealt with King Saul and Goliath. And it wasn't long before I felt someone tugging on the leg of my jeans. I looked down, and David was about to burst into tears.

Leap to page 106

'What am I supposed to do, now?' she whimpered, the panic building.

I tried to calm her down. 'It's OK!' I said. 'You're doing fine.' But she still looked really nervous. At one time, I would have simply asked her if she wanted someone else to play the part. But that can be harmful, too. It wasn't her fault that I'd left her on her own for so long. So instead I asked her if she wanted someone else to come up and help her. As it happened, there were two red-headed twin girls sitting right near the front. They were a little older than her, they were obviously her friends, so she asked if they could come up and play David, too. So, suddenly, David was not one girl, but three! Not historically accurate, but it worked. As a matter of fact, it worked incredibly well! She regained her confidence, her friends supported her, and when they repeated David's lines in unison, it was brilliant!

> 'Relationships with people are more important than the story.'

It was that relationship thing again. The story is important, yes. You want to tell it and tell it well. But the people who participate in the story are more important still. So if you have to stop things, or alter things, or even have a three-headed king of Israel to make somebody feel better, then that's what you do. Because participation creates possibilities that go beyond the power of the story itself.

I have seen this happen many times, but one occasion stands out in particular. It happened near the end of a storytelling session. I needed a boy to come to the front and act out a part, and I chose a little guy sitting right at the back. The teachers gasped a little when I pointed to him. (I get that a lot, actually. The cheeky attitude that can cause so much trouble in class is often perfect when someone has to play a part. I don't know how many times that teachers have told me afterwards, 'You picked the naughtiest kid in the school!') Anyway, I pointed to this child, the teachers gasped, and then he came up and did a great job. Afterwards, during lunch, the teachers told me about him. It turns out that the reason they gasped was not because he was naughty, but because he was terrified of standing in front of a crowd. He had cried right through the school Christmas play, and they were worried that being up front during the story would have the same effect. Well, it didn't. And I would like to think that the secure and joyous environment that we were all a part of in that storytelling event had helped that little boy to find a way past his fears. Yes, participation is great. It makes any story better. But if it can help somebody in the audience, too, then that's the best thing of all!

Choosing Volunteers

So how do you choose a volunteer, when the participation activity requires an individual and not the whole group doing the same thing together? As I said earlier, you start by looking for that cheeky expression or that smiling face. Ideally, you want a volunteer who really wants to be in front of the crowd – someone who will enjoy the moment and help others enjoy it, too. Sometimes the crowd itself gives you a clue. One child will have her hand up and others around her will be pointing at her, as well. That's often a good choice, because the others think she's funny, or popular, and want to see her up there. This is especially true when it comes to choosing teachers as volunteers. When Tim and I did our assembly programmes, we always built a place into the story where we would need a teacher to come up to the front. Kids love to see their teachers doing silly, ridiculous things. But you have to be careful. We made sure that our teacher-participation time was somewhere in the middle of the story. That gave us time to look around – to see which teachers were really enjoying themselves – because we wanted to go for someone who was a good sport. Again, the children would often make the choice for us. We'd ask for a teacher's help and all fingers would point to one man or one woman. It's not that the

'Choose your volunteers carefully.'

kids wanted to see someone humiliated. They seldom knew what was coming, anyway. Instead, they knew who would be fun! They knew who made them laugh. And that's who they wanted to see up front.

What if no one volunteers? Then you do a little coaxing, have a little fun, and assure the crowd that the activity won't be difficult. And if you're still stuck, you can ask two people to do one job (like our little David who needed that added security), offer to do it yourself, or just take a chance and pick someone who's been smiling all along (even if their hand's not in the air!). Sometimes you get lucky and that little extra coaxing does the trick. And then, of course, once the rest of the audience sees that the volunteers are having fun, you have much less trouble getting someone next time round.

Have I made some bad choices through the years? Sure, it's inevitable. There have been the odd occasions (some truly odd!), where volunteers have refused to do certain things, or frozen, or been so wild and over the top that it was difficult to control them. And then there was that teacher – just the one, amazingly – who told me exactly what I could do with my participation activity! But, remember, this was over a twelve-year period, in front of hundreds of thousands of people. And in most of those stories, the participation went very well indeed. Yes, using volunteers is a risk. But it's one I'd take any day, because when it works, it brings an element of freshness and variety and surprise into the stories that would not otherwise be there. And, as I think I have demonstrated, it has the potential to do so many positive things for the participants themselves.

Last, But Not Least
Here are a couple more participation 'tips'.

Always be friendly and encouraging. I like to ask the name of the person who has come to the front and shake his or her hand. It helps to make that person feel more comfortable, I think, and lets him or her know that he or she is more than a moving 'prop'. It also makes it easier to refer to that person by name if something unusually fun happens, or you want to remark on the 'performance' in one way or another. And I do think that each 'performance' should elicit some remark – a clap at the very least, a 'well done', or something more, if what happened was really special. Sometimes you find that you relate really well to the volunteer, and he or she feels free to comment, and you do, too – and a little repartee develops. That's fine, as long as the rest of the audience isn't left out – as long as it continues to serve the story. It's back to the basics again – relationships and playing. If that's what's going on up front with the volunteers, then everyone will have a better time.

> 'Always be friendly and encouraging.'

The same rule applies to individuals as it does to groups – make sure that the participation is simple and interesting. If there are 'lines' to repeat, break them into little chunks – make them easy. If it's an action, make it clear what you want the volunteer to do. And if there is any difficulty, put the volunteer first. Always give that person the chance to step down gracefully if he or she doesn't feel comfortable.

Practising the Story

I like to be on my own when I practise a story. I tell it to myself over and over again, not so much to memorize it word by word, but to make sure that I am thoroughly familiar with it.

I pay particular attention to those places where I intend to inject a participation activity. How will I introduce it? At the start? When I get to that point in the story? And how do I avoid disrupting the flow?

I also pay a lot of attention to any repetition devices. After all, repetition only works if it's repeated! So it's very important to remember where you're planning to use them.

I do all of this until I feel comfortable with the story and have the confidence to stand in front of a crowd and at least look as if I know what I'm doing! However, no matter how much I prepare, the fact of the matter is that with a new story, I'm never really sure how it will 'work' until I try it. I have enough experience to make a good guess, but until I hear an audience laugh at what I assumed would be the funny bits, and join in with what I thought would be the participation bits, and stay dead quiet at what I hoped would be the tense or serious or weepy bits, I can never really be sure. That's the true test – and because I'm working in situations where I can tell the same stories over and over again, I always know I'll get another shot at it! That's reassuring, in itself, and an incentive to stick with a story and improve it, even if things don't work perfectly the first time. What is exciting is to watch a good story mature, grow and develop, until it works really well.

> 'Practise your story over and over again.'

Maybe you're not in that situation. Maybe you have to tell stories to the same audience – in school, or Sunday school – week after week, and there isn't the chance to do the same story twice. The same principles apply to that situation, too. No, you can't watch a single story develop through time – but you have a better chance to get to know your audience, and therefore to experience some sense of development and maturity in the storytelling relationship itself. As you learn what your regular audience thinks is funny or sad or interesting, you develop a sense of confidence from that, as well. So you will know when you've found a story that will really work with that particular group. In my church work, I have certainly found that to be the case when it comes to preaching to the same congregation week after week. And I think it is also true of storytelling.

Finally, you may well be no good at memorizing, at all. Let me assure you then, that if you read a text over and over again, and find some participation activities to get the audience involved, and simply become very familiar with your story, you can get away with using a book. It's not ideal, granted. You do lose some flexibility, in terms of the use of your hands and eyes. But it can be done, and done well. And if that's what you need to feel confident, particularly at first, then try it. Although I suspect that it won't be long before you will want to put the book down!

Leap to page 108

I hope that this section has helped you to see that the right kind of preparation and practice is essential for effective storytelling. Yes, it takes time and effort, but it's well worth it in terms of the quality of the stories you tell. And what's more, it's fun! I love being in front of a group of people. But I also love that moment when a good storytelling 'hook' or 'device' comes to me alone in my study! I can't wait to try it out. And if it's a good one, then the time and the thought and the struggle are all forgotten – replaced by the satisfaction I feel when the story goes down well, and by the look on the faces of the listeners, too. The look you only get when a story has been well told.

4
Retelling Bible Stories

When we were kids, my brothers and I used to take turns spending the weekend with our Grandma Brosi. As is often the case with grandparents, she would let us do all the things that our mum and dad forbade. This included consuming large quantities of sweets, fizzy drinks and sugared cereals. And, best of all, staying up well past our bedtime on a Saturday night. Our usual bedtime was eight o'clock. Grandma, however, would always let us stay up and watch 'Chiller Theater', which didn't even start until the late-night news had finished at eleven!

Chiller Theater was a Pittsburgh institution. It was hosted by a local TV personality, dressed up like Dracula, and featured both some of the best and some of the cheesiest black and white horror films. We'd sit there in the dark, chewing on sweets, gulping down Cokes and scaring ourselves silly before crawling reluctantly into bed. The next morning, Grandma Brosi would teach our Sunday School class – and, somehow, all that creepy stuff from the night before would find its way into the Bible stories that she told. Battles were brilliant! Evil kings were really nasty! And I can't even begin to describe the way in which she detailed the demise of wicked Queen Jezebel! What I can say, though, is that those stories stuck. To this day, I can remember how she told us about the tenth Egyptian plague – the death of the firstborn – and then looked around the room, at those of us who were the oldest in our families, and solemnly said, 'That would be you. And you. And you!'

All right, perhaps a psychologist would have a field day with that approach, and an educational expert would cringe. But it was great drama! And I have never forgotten those stories.

The Fourth Relationship

Biblical storytelling can do one of two things. It can excite and inspire and create a thirst for more. Or it can bore and embarrass and leave a group with a sad sense of 'so what?' And that's an important difference if you believe, as I do, that those stories contain something essential about who we are and who God is.

What is that essential thing? It's the fourth relationship.

Storytelling is about relationships – remember? The relationship between the storyteller and the crowd. The relationship that is built with the characters. The relationship that creates and sustains some sense of community. But when it comes to biblical storytelling, there is always the possibility of a fourth relationship – the relationship with God himself. For I believe that God reveals himself through story.

'Storytelling from the Bible is sacred stuff.'

If you were to ask an ancient Israelite to tell you about God, it is unlikely that he would share some abstract philosophy with you. He might recite a psalm. He might show you a few rules. But it's more likely that he would tell you a story:

'My father Abraham was a wandering Aramean. God called him and promised him that if Abraham would follow him, God would give him a land of his own and descendants to outnumber the stars in the sky or the sands in the sea.'

Or she might say, 'My people were slaves in Egypt. But God set them free and led them to a land flowing with milk and honey!'

The God of Israel is revealed in the story of Israel. We discover who God is by watching how he deals with his people. God's creative power, his passion for justice and his patient steadfast love are all revealed in that story.

And when he chose to reveal himself fully, what did God do? Did he drop an essay down from heaven? Did he pass out a theological tract? No, the Bible tells us he came in the person of one man – Jesus – who was not just a good storyteller, but who was, himself, the Story. So that, by watching what he did, and listening to what he said, people could understand what God was like.

That means that biblical storytelling is quite sacred stuff. And quite powerful, too! It's not just a matter of standing in front of a group of kids and hoping to survive the following fifteen minutes. No, that Sunday school room, that school hall, that slot in the middle of the family service – that is sacred ground! For it is an opportunity for God to do what he has done from the start of his relationship with his people – to reveal himself, to show who he is and what he can do – through the story that you tell!

How Do You Go About It?

So how do you tell biblical stories?

First of all, you start by reading the story in the Bible itself! I know that sounds obvious, but you would be surprised at how often people overlook this first and most important step. I think it comes partly from an over-familiarity that many of us have with certain Bible stories.

'Oh, yeah, that one. I've heard it a hundred times!' And that may be the case. But it never hurts to have another look at even the most familiar story. Because that look might help you spot a detail, a nuance or a new insight that will provide you with a different, original, and unique 'way in' to that story.

Take the story of Jonah, for example. It definitely falls into the 'familiar' category. A 'no-brainer', if there ever was one: God tells him to go to Nineveh. Jonah goes the other way. He gets tossed off the ship and swallowed by a whale. And when he gets spat out on the shore again, he finally does what God tells him.

The only problem is that if you actually read the story, it's not a whale at all – but a big fish (which changes the setting, at the very least!). And while it may look on the surface as if the story is about obedience and disobedience – a closer inspection (particularly of that bit at the end) reveals that 'Jonah' is actually all about racism. That's right – racism! Because Jonah's disobedience is due to the fact that he hates the people of Nineveh and does not want God to save them. That's why he sits on the hill at the end and watches over the city. He's waiting – waiting for them to fall back into their evil ways, in the hope that God will destroy them after all. So what does God do? He makes a tree grow over Jonah to give him shade. And then he sends a worm to kill the tree. And when Jonah complains that the tree is dead, God brings him face to face to with his upside-down priorities. 'You care about this tree,' God sighs. 'But you care nothing for a city full of people who

'Read the original story in the Bible before you start.'

do not know their right hand from their left.' And that's where the story ends! We never even get to hear Jonah's response. Why? Because the original storyteller – the person who wrote the book of Jonah – wanted the reader, wanted the hearer, to provide his or her own response. Will we love those whom God loves (even though they are different, even though they are our enemies)? Or will we continue in our prejudice and hate?

Leap to page 110

It's a powerful story, Jonah. But it's even more powerful (and surely more appropriate to our day and age) if you take the time to take a closer look.

Find the Hook

Having re-read the Bible story, I break it down as usual and try to find a hook to hang the story on to make it more memorable.

Sometimes that hook is there among the characters. When I retold David and Goliath in *The Lion Storyteller Bible*, I saw it in terms of 'little', 'bigger', and 'big'. Who are the three main characters, after all? David, who is little. King Saul, who is bigger. And Goliath, who is very big indeed! This very simple device not only gave me a way to describe the characters, but also helped to state the problem, and, as a really big bonus, left me with a natural 'group of three' to set the pace! It's not always that easy, of course, but you will be surprised at how many 'ways in' you can find if you take just a little time to pull the story apart.

Leap to page 106

You can find hooks in settings as well. As I read through the story of Joshua and the battle of Jericho, the thing that jumped out at me was the fact that he and his followers had to march around the walls. So the phrase 'round and round' became the hook to tie the story together. The walls go 'round and round' the city. Joshua's thoughts spin 'round and round' in his head. The angel's sword (a detail, I confess, I didn't even know until I read the story carefully!) swings 'round and round' his head. The soldiers gather 'round and round' to hear the plan. And, last of all, the people, at last, march 'round and round' till the walls come tumbling down. It's simple, I know! But as I've suggested many times already, it's

Leap to page 112

usually the simplest ideas that are the best. And when they are connected to the setting, they also help, I think, to make the story more real, more concrete.

Find the Problem

As with all retellings, you need to discover the story's main problem. Sometimes, particularly with biblical stories, that's not as easy as it may seem. I've described some of the difficulties in an earlier chapter (too many problems for one sitting, more than one problem to choose from), but let me use one story to illustrate how thinking through the problem can help you find a 'way in' as well. In the Gospel story where the man is lowered through the roof by his friends, there are two problems. There is the man's need to get to Jesus – which his friends solve by tearing up their neighbour's roof so that their friend can be healed. But there is also the theological controversy that erupts between Jesus and the religious leaders when Jesus tells the man that his sins are forgiven. When I retold this story in *The Lion Storyteller Bible*,

Leap to page 114

I suppose that I could simply have ignored the second problem. The difficulty, though, is that the two problems are very closely connected – Jesus heals the man to demonstrate

63

that he has the authority to forgive his sins. The solution I came up with was to create a character – the daughter of one of the religious leaders – to serve as a set of eyes for the reader. She was then able to look objectively at the situation as it developed, and also ask the kinds of questions that any child might: Why is someone tearing a hole in the roof? Will Jesus be able to help the man? Why is my father so angry at what Jesus is saying? In a sense, the main problem becomes 'What's going on here?', but the other problems get solved along the way, and the reader/listener is given someone specific to whom they can relate. And, best of all, I believe the original intention of the story is preserved.

How Far Can We Go?

I think that being faithful to the original story is incredibly important when it comes to biblical storytelling. We can invent new characters, insert new details, ask questions of the text and fill in some of the gaps between the lines. But it is important that we are faithful to what we understand to be the intent of that particular story. And it is also important, I think, that we are faithful to the facts that we have already been given. I will readily admit that I have filled some of the gaps with a certain amount of imagination. And I have had plenty of conversations with people who were not comfortable

with that. My response was that they should work to their own comfort level, as far as gaps in the story are concerned. Some tellers will not want to stray from the text at all. That's fine. But I also think there is room for some 'sanctified imagining' between the gaps, particularly if that creativity helps to open up the story for someone.

But what if your listeners go back to the Bible and they discover that the story isn't just like you told it? That's a fair question, and all I can suggest is that we are honest about what we're doing. In the preface to *Angels, Angels All Around* I tried to make clear exactly what I was doing and why. And I preface those stories in the same way when I tell them.

Leap to page 81

'Here's the story of Daniel in the Lions' Den,' I say. 'You may have heard it before, but I'm going to tell it in a different way. I'm going to glue it together with that game you might have played – What's the Time, Mr Wolf? – and we're going to see what happens!'

The only story that I can honestly say does not conform to these principles is my re-telling of the little-known story of Ehud and King Eglon in *Bible Baddies*. The original story is just a few verses and simply describes how Ehud was called as a 'judge' to deliver the people of Israel from one of their enemies. At the time I wrote the story, however, I was struggling with some of the more violent parts of the Old Testament and

Leap to page 116

effectively developed a story around the story of Ehud to explore the repercussions of that violence. Again, I explained what I was doing in the introduction, and admit the same thing whenever I tell it. But, looking back on it, this story is probably now on the edge of my comfort zone, as well!

Big gaps or little gaps, the key thing is to tell the story in such a way that it becomes accessible. Accessible to those who've heard it a hundred times, because you have found some creative 'way in'. And accessible to those who have never heard it before.

Just a few months ago, I was taking an RE class at the school across the street. My remit was to talk with the class about the reasons Christians behave the way they do – how they decide what is right and what is wrong. I told them that Christians are people who follow Jesus. So we try to do the things he did. I asked them if they knew any good things that Jesus did.

One girl said that he healed people. A boy said that Jesus fed people who were hungry. So we talked about the ways that we could do those things now. And then a little boy at the back put up his hand.

'Didn't Jesus die by being crushed under a big rock?' he asked.

I thought about that for a moment.

'No,' I said. 'He did die, but he didn't die that way. You might be thinking about what happened three days after he died. Do you know what happened?' I asked. And the little boy shook his head.

'Well,' I went on, 'when Jesus died, they buried him in a tomb, a grave, and rolled a big stone in front of it. And three days later, when the stone was rolled away, Jesus wasn't there any more. Jesus was alive.'

The little boy looked at me, and I promise you, this is what he did. His mouth hung open and all he said was, 'Wow!'

That's the reaction I want to get when I tell a Bible story. I want to get a 'Wow!' Because, you see, that's the kind of reaction that Peter or Paul or any of those early followers of Jesus got when they told that same story for the very first time. Told it to people like that little boy – people who had never heard it before. For when those first Christians told the story (and when they did their best to live it, as well!), the people who heard it didn't just have a pleasant time and finish with polite applause – they went, 'Wow!', they entered into some kind of relationship with God, and their lives (not to mention the world in which they lived) were changed for ever.

The Last Word

Seven words. That's all it takes. And smiles break out on faces, hands clap their approval, it's the end. 'And they all lived happily ever after.'

We've come to the end here, as well. And, because I am a great believer in those happy endings, there is just one last thing I would like to say: 'Go tell someone a story!'

I attend a lot of conferences where I teach exactly the kinds of things you have been reading about in this book. Sometimes, I even get invited back the following year. And the very best thing that happens is when someone comes up to me that second year and says, 'I tried it. I did it! I took what you taught me and now I'm telling stories!'

That would be the very best conclusion to this book, as well – if you would take what you have learned and try it out on some assembly, Sunday school class, congregation, youth group, group of friends or maybe even just one single child at bedtime.

So, go play! Go build relationships! Go have some fun! Go tell a story! And may the telling take you to those 'happily ever after' places as well!

Top Storytelling Tips

- The heart of good storytelling is PLAY. Imagine yourself back to when you were a child and you made up imaginary worlds.

- Get lots of eye-contact with your audience.

- Set some simple ground-rules with the children before you start: for example, 'When I hold up my hand I want you to be really quiet.'

- Practise different voices.

- Practise different expressions: lock yourself up in the bathroom and look in the mirror. Throw yourself into it 100%. Don't hold back!

- Find an intriguing or fun 'way in' to the story.

- Think carefully about your characters.

- Choose your setting (make it easy for the children to imagine).

- Find a good, clear central problem (the way the characters resolve the problem is the thing that keeps the audience hooked).

- Use repetition. Keep coming back to some phrases throughout the story. They will keep the children's attention and help you keep the flow, too.

- Get your audience to participate.

- Don't be afraid to give it a go, and have fun!

The Stories

The Big Spender

Here's a retelling of the story of the Prodigal Son. It's the story that a woman in my first church found herself relating to in a way that I did not expect. (See page 15.)

The people who thought they were good were still not happy with Jesus. They moaned. They grumbled. They frowned.

'It's not fair,' they complained. 'Jesus spends all his time with the bad people.'

Jesus heard this and told them one more story:

'Once upon a time there was a man who had two sons. He loved them both, very much. But one day, the younger son came to him with a sad request.

' "Father," the younger son said, "when you die, I will get part of your money and part of your land. The problem is, I don't want to wait. I want my money now!"

'It was all the father could do to hold back his tears. But because he loved his son, he agreed, and gave him his share of the money.

'That very day the son left home, money in his pocket and a big smile on his face. He didn't even say goodbye. The father just watched, wiped away a tear, and hoped that one day he would see his son again.

'The son travelled to a country far, far away and spent his money just as fast as he could. He drank. He gambled. He used his money to do many bad things – until finally the money was gone.

'The son looked for a job, but the only work he could find was taking care of pigs! It was hard, dirty work, and he was so hungry sometimes he thought about taking the pigs' food for himself. He was miserable, lonely and sad. And then one day, he had an idea.

' "The servants who take care of my father's animals are much happier than me. I'll go home, that's what I'll do. I'll tell my father how sorry I am for wasting his money. And maybe, just maybe, he'll let me become a servant and work for him."

'Now what do you think the father had been doing all this time? Did he say to himself, "I have my eldest son at home with me. Who cares if my younger son is gone?" Of course not! He loved his son, even though he had gone far away. And every day, he would go out to the roadside and watch, hoping his son would return.

'That's exactly where he was when the younger son hobbled home, poor and hungry. The father ran to his son and hugged him tight. And the son dropped right to his knees.

' "Oh, Father," he cried. "I'm so sorry. I have wasted all your money and am no longer good enough to be your son."

' "Don't be silly," said the father. "You are my son. You will always be my son. And I am so glad to have you back!" Then the father lifted his son to his feet and walked him home. He dressed him in beautiful clothes. He put gold rings on his fingers. And he threw him a big welcome home party.

'When the elder son came home from work that night, he heard the party noise.

' "What's happening?" he asked. And when a servant told him, he was filled with anger and ran to his father.

' "It's not fair!" he shouted. "I've been a good son. I've worked hard for you all these years. But he was bad. He wasted your money. And now you're throwing him a party."

' "I love you, my son," the father said. "And you have enjoyed all the good things I have. But your brother was gone, and now he's back. He was lost, and now he's found. That's why I'm having this party, because we're all back together again."

From *The Lion Storyteller Bible*, text copyright © 1995 Bob Hartman

The Steel Man

This is a version of the very first story my brother and I told when we worked for the Pittsburgh Children's Museum. It's still one of my favourites. (See page 16.)

One by one, the steel-working men huffed and puffed and struggled to lift the long steel beams. It was a contest – a contest that took place once a year in the smoky shadow of the steel mill – to prove who was the strongest man in the steel-making valley.

But as the light of the setting sun mingled with the blast-furnace soot and fire, not a man among them had yet been able to lift the heaviest beam of all.

Suddenly they heard something – Boom! Boom! Boom! Then they felt the earth shake. And finally, they saw him, tramping through the twilight, hammering the ground with his steel-tipped shoes – a giant of a man, nine feet tall at least, with hands like shovels and a head full of burnt brown hair!

He lumbered through the crowd, right up to the heaviest steel beam. Then he wrapped one hairy fist around it – and swung it up over his head!

The crowds gasped. They had never seen anyone so strong. But the big man just tilted back his head and laughed – a rumbling, tumbling sound, like steel makes as it bubbles and boils in the furnace.

'Let me introduce myself,' he roared. 'My father was the sun, hotter than any furnace. My mother was Mother Earth herself. And I was born in the belly of an ore-bearing mountain. For I am a man who is made of steel! And my name is Joe Magarac.'

Now it was the crowd's turn to laugh. For in their language, the word 'magarac' meant 'donkey'!

'Laugh all you want,' the big man chuckled. 'Because all I want to do is eat like a donkey and work like a donkey!'

The steel-working men laughed again, and clapped and cheered. Then they gathered round Joe and introduced themselves.

But high in the steel mill, in the fancy room where the bosses worked, there was another man – the Big Boss, the man who owned the steel mill. His face was pressed to the window and, through the grime and the smoke, he could see what was going on in the yard below.

'He's a strong man.' The Big Boss smiled. 'So I will hire him to work for me. Then maybe I won't need to hire so many other men.'

Joe started every day in the same way. He gobbled up a bucket of coal, and washed it down with a bowl of steaming, hot steel soup. Then he tramped over to the mill, picking his teeth with a hard, cold chisel.

He grabbed a pile of old railroad tracks with one arm, and ten tons of iron ore with the other. Then he carried them over to the Furnace Number Nine and dumped them in. And finally he shovelled coal underneath and set the whole thing burning with a finger-snap spark.

The stuff inside the furnace started to melt. It turned red and orange and yellow and white hot. But that heat didn't bother Joe. No, he stuck his arm in there and stirred it around. 'Kind of tickles,' he laughed.

And then, as that stuff cooled down, thick and gooey, Joe grabbed a handful in his fist and squeezed it tight. And out between his fingers oozed four perfect steel beams!

Day by day, week by week, month by month, those beams piled up. Until the warehouses were full. And the steel yard. And, at last the mill itself.

And that's when the Big Boss came down from his fancy room.

'Boys!' he hollered. 'I got some bad news for you. Joe Magarac, here, has made so much steel, we're not gonna need any more for a while. So I want you to go home. I'll call you if I want you to work again.'

73

The steel-working men walked slowly home. No work meant no money. And that meant no food on the table or shoes on their children's feet.

They turned and looked back at the mill. No furnace firelight dancing against the window-panes. No clouds billowing black out of the smoke-stacks. Nothing but stillness and sadness and rust.

And inside the mill there was only Joe, sitting in Furnace Number Nine, a little steel tear running down his big steel cheek.

'This is my fault,' he whispered to the dirty walls. 'I ate like a donkey and worked like a donkey, and now my friends have no jobs. I must do something to help them.'

The clocks in the houses of the steel-working men ticked away hours and days and weeks and months. Their families were hungry. Their hopes were fading. And then, one night, just as the clock struck nine, they saw it, down in the valley – a furnace burning in the mill!

They rushed out of their houses and down the crooked hillside streets. They burst into the mill itself. And that's when they heard it – the very same sound they'd heard on the night that Joe came tramping through the twilight – the rumbling, tumbling sound that steel makes as it bubbles and boils in the furnace.

They followed that sound, and it led them to Furnace Number Nine. And there, in the furnace, was the head of Joe Magarac, floating on a white-hot pool of steel.

'Joe! Get out of there!' they shouted.

But Joe just laughed. 'Don't worry about me,' he said. 'I was the reason you lost your jobs. And now I'm gonna fix that. When I am all melted down, I want you to pour me out into steel beams, 'cause my steel is the strongest steel there is. Then I want you to tear down this old mill and use my beams to make a new one. A bigger one. One that will make jobs for you and your children for years to come!'

The big man said, 'Goodbye!' and then the head of Joe Magarac disappeared into the boiling steel and he was never seen again.

The men did what Joe told them, and the next year there was

another strong man contest in the new steel yard. And the prize? It was the privilege of tending the fires in Furnace Number Nine – the furnace where Joe Magarac had sacrificed himself for everyone in the steel-making valley.

The Big Wave

This is one of my favourite 'community-building' stories. It's also the story that a little girl told me she could 'see'. (See page 19.)

The sea splashed gently against the sandy beach. The sandy beach lay white and hot before the little village. And in the little village lived four hundred people – old men and young men, mothers and grandmothers, babies and boys and girls.

Behind the village, green terraces rose like steps to a high, flat plateau. And on the plateau stood a fine old house, surrounded by rice fields.

In that house lived Hamaguchi – an old man, a rich man, owner of the rice fields and lord of the village below. With him lived his grandson – only ten years old, full of questions and full of life.

One hot summer evening, Hamaguchi walked slowly out onto his porch. He looked at the village below, and smiled. It was harvest time, and his people were celebrating with music and dancing and bright lantern lights.

He looked at the beach beyond, cool and quiet and calm, and he smiled again.

But when Hamaguchi looked out across the sea, his smile turned suddenly to a worried frown. For there was a wave, a wave that stretched as far as he could see, tall and wild and fierce. And it was rushing towards the village below.

Hamaguchi had never seen this kind of wave. But he had heard tales about such waves from his father and his father's father. So he called his grandson and asked him to bring a flaming torch.

'Why, Grandfather?' the boy asked, innocently. 'Why do you want a torch?'

'There is no time to explain,' Hamaguchi answered. 'We must act quickly!' And he hobbled to the fields on the left of the house and set his crops on fire.

'Grandfather!' the boy cried. 'What are you doing?'

Hamaguchi looked down at the village. No one was looking up at the plateau.

'There is no time!' he barked. 'Come with me.' And he took the boy by the hand and set fire to the fields on the right.

The flames burst orange and yellow and white against the night, and the boy began to weep.

'Grandfather, are you mad? This is everything you own!'

But the old man said nothing. He looked down at the village, then hurried to the remaining fields and set the torch to them, as well. The sky was filled with sparks and smoke and the little boy was sobbing now.

'Please, Grandfather! Stop, Grandfather! There will be nothing left!'

Just then, a bell sounded, ringing from the temple in the village below. And soon, streaming up the terraced hill, came the villagers – young women, old women, boys and girls, fathers and grandfathers, babies on their backs and buckets in their hands. All four hundred of them – running to help put out the fire!

And, just as they reached the burning fields, the wave struck the village below.

It sounded like thunder.

It sounded like cannon fire.

It sounded like the hoof-beats of ten thousand horses.

It destroyed everything in its path, and when at last it rumbled and rolled back out to sea, there was not a single house left standing.

The people looked in horror at the ruins of their village. But when at last they turned to face the fields, they were gone as well – burned to the ground.

Hamaguchi's grandson grabbed him round the waist and, sobbing still, asked the question everyone else wanted to hear.

'Why, Grandfather? Why did you burn down your precious fields?'

'Don't you see?' the old man said to the crowd. 'I had to find some way to warn you – to lead you out of harm's way. For, as precious as my fields are to me, each and every one of you is more precious still.'

And with that, Hamaguchi invited them to all stay in his house until the village was rebuilt.

The old man lived many more years, but when, at last, he died, the people built a little shrine in their village, in memory of the lord who sacrificed all he had to save them from the terrible wave.

The Crocodile Brother

Here's another good 'community-building' story. (See page 28.)

Once upon a time, there were two tribes who simply could not get along with each other. It started with a stolen cow, then a few missing pigs. Hard words followed, then threats. And when the eldest son of one of the chiefs was found murdered, everyone prepared for war!

The father of the murdered boy was broken-hearted. But in spite of his anger and his grief, the last thing he wanted was for other fathers to lose their sons as well. So he persuaded the elders of both tribes to come together and try to work out some peaceful solution.

At first, the meeting looked certain to fail. It started with suspicious stares and soon turned into ugly shouting.

But just before the meeting fell apart completely, the chief stood and raised his hands in the air and cried, 'Crocodile!'

Everyone fell silent, each head turning this way and that, looking for the beast. And this gave the chief a chance to speak.

'There is no crocodile among us,' he said softly. 'Not yet, at least. But listen to my story, brothers, please. And perhaps you will see what I mean.

'Once there lived a crocodile,' the chief began, 'who spotted a tasty fat chicken by the side of the river. The crocodile grinned. The crocodile opened its mouth wide. The crocodile showed its rows of sharp white teeth. But just before the crocodile snapped its jaws shut around its prey, the chicken spoke!

' "My brother," begged the chicken, "please spare my life. Find something else for your supper."

'These words surprised the crocodile. My brother? he wondered. What does the chicken mean by that? And while he wondered, the chicken slipped away.

'The next day, the crocodile spied a sleek, juicy duck. The crocodile grinned. The crocodile opened its mouth wide. The crocodile showed its rows of sharp, white teeth. But just before the crocodile snapped its jaws shut around its prey, the duck spoke!

' "My brother," begged the duck, "please spare my life. Find something else for your supper."

'Again the crocodile was shocked. Brother? he wondered. When did I become brother to a chicken and a duck? And as he tried to puzzle it out, the duck slipped away.

'The crocodile was confused. And he was getting hungrier by the hour. So he went to see his friend, the lizard. He told him about the chicken, and he told him about the duck. And as he did so, the lizard nodded and smiled.

' "I understand completely!" answered the lizard. "For I am your brother, too!"

' "My brother?" cried the crocodile. "How?"'

' "I was hatched from an egg," replied the lizard. "And so was the chicken and so was the duck." And then he smiled at the crocodile. "And so, my brother, were you! When you think about it, we are more alike than we ever imagined. So why should we want to eat each other?"'

His story finished, the chief turned to the elders.

'My brothers,' he said, 'we are just like that crocodile.'

'Nonsense!' called out one of the elders. 'I was never hatched from any egg!' And the elders on both sides laughed.

'No,' grinned the chief. 'But you have eyes and ears and hands and feet, as we all do. And a son – as many of us have as well. We are more alike than we ever imagined. So why should we devour one another in war, when we can live together like brothers in peace?'

From *The Lion Storyteller Book of Animal Tales*, text copyright © 2002 Bob Hartman

Dinner in the Lions' Den

Here's another example of playing with a story and finding a 'way in'. Is every angel the same? I don't think so. And it was great fun weaving in the 'Mr Wolf Game' as well! (See pages 30 and 65.)

King Darius did not want to dump Daniel into the lions' den. And Daniel certainly did not want to be dumped there. But a law was a law – even if the king had been tricked into making it. And Daniel had broken the law by praying to God when the law said he shouldn't.

While Daniel's enemies were laughing and slapping each other on the back for tricking the king, two things happened at almost the same time.

King Darius sent up a prayer, like a small white bird, to ask Daniel's God to protect Daniel.

And Daniel sent up a small white bird of his own.

It did not take long for God to send an answer back. But it might have seemed long to Daniel as he was lowered into the lions' den.

There were four lions in the den. A huge father lion with a shaggy brown mane. A sleek mother lion with golden brown hair. And two tumbling and not quite grown-up cubs.

The lions looked at Daniel and drooled. Their bellies growled as only lion bellies can.

'He's skinny,' said Father Lion, 'and scrawny and old.'

'He'll be tough,' said Mother Lion, 'but tasty.'

'Dibs on the drumsticks!' said one of the cubs.

When Daniel looked at the lions, all he saw were four open mouths and four sets of sharp, white teeth. And all Daniel heard was a rising, roaring chorus as the lions padded closer.

Suddenly, something like a curtain seemed to open between heaven and earth. 'Wait just a minute!' called a voice through the opening. God's answer had arrived.

It was an angel. An angel who was good with lions. An angel who looked a bit like a lion himself. A great, stocky, slab-footed angel with hulking hands and a shaggy brown head of hair.

'It's not time for that yet,' called the angel.

'Oh?' growled Father Lion. 'Then what time is it, Mr Angel?'

The angel paused for a moment and thought. 'It's scratching time,' he said.

Then the angel laid one huge hand on Father's Lion's head and started scratching behind his ears. Those chunky fingers felt good, and Father Lion stopped his growling, laid himself down and began to purr. With his other hand, the angel scratched Mother Lion at the base of her neck where it met her shoulders. Soon she was purring, too.

'Me next! Me next!' shouted the cubs. And for a long time, Daniel heard nothing but scratching and purring and mewing.

Then one of the lions' tummies started to growl again. And Father Lion glanced at Daniel through his mane, rolled his tongue out across his lips and showed the end of one white fang.

'What time is it now, Mr Angel?' he asked.

'It's belly-rubbing time, of course,' answered the angel.

Father Lion muttered a disappointed 'Oh,' but the other members of his family were quite excited.

'Me first!' mewed one of the cubs.

'You were first last time,' mewed the other.

'There'll be turns for everyone,' said the angel as he turned over a cub with each hand. Then he smiled at Daniel and winked.

And then... you know how it is with belly rubbing. First you're rubbing bellies and then you're wrestling. If any of Daniel's enemies had found the courage to put his ear to the stone on top of the den, he would have thought that old Daniel was being torn to pieces. But it was only the lions rolling and biting and pawing at each other as they played 'Trap the Tail' and 'Cuff the Cub'. And that great, tawny angel was playing hardest of all.

When they had finished, the lions collapsed, exhausted, on the floor of their den.

'What time is it? What time is it now, Mr Angel?' yawned Father Lion.

The angel stretched wide his arms, shook his shaggy head and yawned back, 'It's sleepy time, I think.'

And the lions curled up like housecats in front of a fire and were soon fast asleep. The angel curled up with them, wrapping his long, lionlike self around them. But he kept one eye open, just in case.

Next morning everyone in the den was awakened by the crunching, scraping sound of the stone den cover being hastily slid aside.

'Daniel!' The king's voice echoed through the den. 'Daniel! Has your God answered my prayer? Has your God saved you?'

'Yes, Your Majesty, he has indeed.' Daniel's sleepy voice bounced back up into the light. 'God has answered both our prayers. He sent his angel to shut the lions' mouths.'

The delighted king had his servants quickly pull Daniel out of the den. Then they dropped Daniel's enemies – those laughing, back-slapping tricksters – into the den instead.

The lions stretched and stood up and stared. They were wide awake now. And very hungry.

The angel stretched and stood up with them. 'Well, I must go now,' he said. 'Goodbye, lions.'

And then he pulled back that mysterious curtain between heaven and earth and started to step inside.

'Wait!' growled Father Lion. 'Before you go… tell me, Mr Angel, what time is it now?'

The angel looked at Daniel's enemies and the four hungry lions. And he grinned a wide cat grin. Then he drew the curtain around him, leaving only his answer and a shadow of that grin behind.

'What time is it?' said the angel. 'It's dinner time.'

From *Angels, Angels, All Around* © 1993 Bob Hartman

83

The Bully's Tale

This is an example of finding a different 'way in' to a story – the tale of David and Goliath told largely from the giant's point of view. (See page 31.)

He hated little things. And maybe that was because he had never really been little himself.

He had been a baby once, of course. But he was the biggest baby the people of Gath had ever seen! So it was big robes and big sandals and big toys, right from the start. And, 'Don't push that little boy, dear.' And, 'Careful with that pot, child.' And, 'Don't squeeze the kitty so hard, Goliath – you'll hurt him.'

Little things. Little kitties. Little people. The world was full of them! And it didn't take long for them to notice that he was different – and to bring it, constantly, to his attention.

Some children return teasing with humour. Other with sullen stares. But Goliath chose fear. Even the most harmless comment about his size would result in a furious beating from the big boy. Yes, he was beaten up a few times, himself – by some of Gath's older lads. But he soon outgrew them all, and then no one dared challenge the boy who stood nearly seven feet tall!

'There's only one thing to do with bullies…' his father finally said. 'The army! That'll sort him out.'

Given his size and strength, he might have risen high in the ranks. But his obvious hatred for the 'little generals' and their 'little rules' kept him marching with the infantry. In the end, there was only one thing Goliath was good for – frightening the enemy. And he was very good at that indeed!

He'd strap on his armour – all 125 gleaming pounds of it.

Then he'd pick up his spear – 10 feet long, with a ten-pound iron point.

And finally he would stand at the front of the Philistine troops – a shining monster of a man.

'A challenge!' he would roar – and his roar rumbled across the valley to whichever army was camped on the other side. 'A challenge is what I offer! Send your best man to fight me. And if he wins,' and here Goliath always had a little chuckle, 'we shall be your slaves.'

A few men had taken up his challenge. Little men. With little swords. Goliath always smiled when he remembered how he had crushed their little heads and left their little bodies broken and twisted and torn.

Most men, however, never even tried. His presence alone made their little hearts beat with fear and send them retreating to their little tents.

He expected as much today. The Israelites were not just a little people, they were the littlest of them all! A few scattered tribes. A puny, ramshackle army. And if what he had heard was true, they had just one little god to protect them. It hardly seemed worth the trouble, but he marched out anyway into the valley of Elah and issued his customary challenge. He anticipated a short day's work. But he had no idea how short it would turn out to be.

The Israelites heard the challenge, as they had every day for the past forty days. And, to a man, they trembled. But someone else heard the challenge, too. Someone who had never heard it before. And it made him angry.

Maybe it had to do with his feelings about his people. Maybe it had to do with his feelings about his God. Or maybe he was just tired of being little.

David was the youngest of eight brothers, after all. And no matter how much courage he had shown, defending his father's flock of sheep, they all still thought of him as the 'runt'. Hand-me-down sandals and pass-me-down robes – that was his lot. And while his older brothers were able to serve as soldiers, the best he could do was bring them lunch and carry chunks of goat's cheese to their commanders!

'If only,' David dreamed, 'I could do something big, for a change.'

And then he heard Goliath's challenge.

'So what do you get if you beat the giant?' he asked a soldier close by.

'A king's ransom,' the soldier answered. 'And the king's own daughter.'

'Well,' mused David, 'I'm surprised someone hasn't accepted the challenge already.'

And that's when he felt a hand – a big hand – on his shoulder. The hand belonged to his oldest brother, Eliab.

'What are you doing here?' Eliab growled.

'Bread… umm, cheese…' David muttered.

'Excuses, more like it,' Eliab growled again. 'Get back to the fields, where you belong!'

But David did not go back to the fields. No, he crept along the front lines, talking to one soldier after another, always about the giant. Finally, word got back to King Saul, who asked to see the boy.

The giant meanwhile was still waiting.

'Their little hearts are in their little throats,' he chuckled, in a nasty sort of way. Then he looked down at his shield-bearer. The little man was not chuckling back. In fact, it was all he could do, in the hot noonday sun, to keep himself and the shield standing upright.

'Pathetic,' Goliath muttered, and then wondered if the Israelites would ever send him a challenger.

'So you want to fight the giant?' grinned King Saul.

David had seen that look before. He got it from his big brothers all the time. It was that 'I'm-not-taking-you-seriously-you're-just-a-little-shepherd-boy' kind of look.

So David stood as tall as he could and answered with the straightest face and the deepest voice he could manage.

'Yes, Your Majesty, I do.'

'And what makes you think you can beat him?' the king continued, more seriously now.

David didn't even have to think.

'I have fought lions,' he said. 'And I have fought bears. All to save my father's sheep. And every time, the Lord God has helped me win. I am sure he will do the same with this giant.'

The king didn't know what to do. The boy had courage. The boy had faith. But if he allowed him to fight the giant, the boy would also soon be dead! Still, he needed a champion – any champion! So he made the boy an offer.

'My armour,' said the king, pointing to the other side of the tent. 'At least take my armour. My shield. My sword. My breastplate. Whatever you like! You will need all the protection you can get.'

David looked at the armour. He even tried a piece or two of it on. But it was much too big and much too heavy for him.

'I have all the protection I need,' he said to the king, at last. 'The Lord God himself will be my breastplate. He alone will be my shield.' And he bowed and turned and walked out of the tent.

Goliath, meanwhile, was tapping one big foot on the ground and humming an old Philistine folk song.

'In another minute, we're going back to camp,' he said to his shield-bearer, who breathed a relieved sigh and thanked every god he could think of. But before he could finish his prayer, a cheer rang out from the Israelite camp. Someone was walking on to the battlefield.

'At last!' Goliath drooled, like a hungry man who has just been told it's dinnertime.

The figure looked small, at first. Goliath put it down to the distance. But the closer he got, the smaller it seemed, until the giant realized, at last, that his challenger was no more than a boy!

'Is this some kind of a joke?' he muttered to his shield-bearer. But neither the shield-bearer nor the boy was laughing.

'Or is it...' and here the giant's words turned into a snarl, 'is it some kind of Israelite insult? Do they mock me? Do they make fun of me? Well, we'll see who has the last laugh!'

And then he roared – roared so the ground shook, and the shield-bearer, as well.

'Do you think I am a dog?' he roared. 'That you come at me with this little stick of a boy? Send me a real challenger. Or surrender!'

'I am the real challenger,' said David, in that deep voice he had used before the king. 'And the God I serve is the real God. He will give me the victory today!'

Goliath had heard enough. He grabbed his shield and raised his spear and charged. Little people and little generals and little soldiers. Little things had plagued him all his life! And now this little boy and his little army and his pathetic little god were going to pay. He'd skewer the lad and crush his little head and show everyone what someone big and strong could do!

But as he rushed towards the boy, David calmly reached into his shepherd's pouch. He placed a small stone into his sling and he swung it round his head. Then he prayed that God would make his throw both strong and true.

The stone and the giant sped towards each other. And at the last moment, Goliath caught a glimpse of it – a tiny speck, a minute fragment, so small it was hardly worth avoiding. But when it struck him between the eyes, he roared and he cried and fell crashing to the ground. And that little thing was the last thing that the giant ever saw!

From *More Bible Baddies*, text copyright © 2001 Bob Hartman

Jesus and the Taxman

What is the 'problem' in the story of Zacchaeus? There are several choices, actually. See if you can spot the choice I made in this retelling. (See page 32.)

'Jesus is coming!' somebody shouted. 'Jesus is coming to Jericho!' And everybody ran to meet him.

Well, almost everybody. For there was one man – one wee little man – who did not run to meet Jesus. And his name was Zacchaeus.

It's not that Zacchaeus didn't want to see Jesus. He did. He really did. But, not only was Zacchaeus short, he was also afraid of the crowd. Not many people liked him, you see. Partly because he was a tax collector. But mostly because he collected more taxes than he was supposed to – and kept what was left for himself.

'Jesus is here!' somebody shouted. 'Jesus is here in Jericho!' And everybody cheered as he walked through the city gates.

Well, almost everybody. For Zacchaeus did not feel like cheering at all. He wanted to see Jesus. He really did. But how could he walk out there in front of all those people he'd cheated? And what would they do if they got hold of him?

Then Zacchaeus had an idea. There were trees by the city gates – tall, leafy trees. If he could sneak behind the crowd and climb one of those trees, he could see Jesus – and not be seen himself!

So off he went – out of his house and through the empty streets. And because the crowd was watching Jesus, he had no trouble at all slipping behind them and shinning up the tree.

'Come, eat at my house!' somebody shouted. 'Come, eat at my house, Jesus!' And because it was a great honour to host someone as important as Jesus, everybody shouted at once.

Well, almost everybody. For there was one man – one wee little man – who kept his mouth shut and tried hard not to rustle the branches.

'Thank you very much,' said Jesus. 'You are very kind. But I have already decided where I will eat my dinner.'

Then Jesus looked straight at the trees and called, 'Zacchaeus! Zacchaeus, come down! I'm eating at your house today.'

'Zacchaeus?' somebody shouted. 'Jesus is eating with Zacchaeus? He's the worst man in town. There must be some mistake!' And everybody moaned and groaned.

Well, almost everybody. One man – one wee little man – climbed down from the tree, as shocked as the rest. Why would someone as good as Jesus want to eat with someone bad like him? But he was happy, too. Happier than he'd been for a long, long time. And so, with a smile spreading across his face, Zacchaeus led Jesus to his house.

'What are they saying?' somebody whispered. 'What are they doing in there?' And everybody gathered around the taxman's door.

That's when Zacchaeus threw open his door with a bang!

'Greetings, everyone!' he shouted. 'I have an announcement to make. I've been talking with my new friend, Jesus, and realize that there are a few things I need to change. I've cheated some of you. I admit that. And I want you to know that I'm sorry. So sorry, in fact, that I will pay you back four times more than I stole from you! What's more, I intend to sell half of what I own and give the money to the poor!'

The crowd was shocked. Never, in their whole lives, had they seen anyone change like that! They stood there with their mouths wide open. And nobody said a thing.

Well, almost nobody.

'Don't you see?' said Jesus to the crowd. 'God has sent me to share his love with everybody – even those who have done some very bad things. That's what I have done. And now Zacchaeus loves God, too.'

That's when the crowd began to cheer. Jesus. And Zacchaeus. And the whole town of Jericho.

Everybody.

From *The Lion Storyteller Bible*, text copyright © 1995 Bob Hartman

The Storm on the Lake

Here's a story that uses the setting to find a 'way in'. You could ask the audience to rock gently back and forth. They are the waves on the lake, and they need to keep rocking throughout the story – gently at first and then more wildly as the storm strikes. Then calm them down, as Jesus stills the storm, and finally make them rock gently again. (See page 34.)

It was a perfect day.

The sky was blue. The lake, too.

And a gentle breeze whipped the wave tips white and foamy.

Jesus sat at the side of the lake and talked to the people about God.

'God is your Father,' he said. 'He dresses the flowers in beautiful colours. He makes sure the birds have enough to eat. But you are his sons and his daughters. Don't you think he can clothe and feed you, too? So trust him, and stop worrying your lives away.'

When Jesus had finished teaching, he was tired. So he called his closest friends, and together they piled into a boat and set off across the lake for home.

Jesus yawned. He stretched. He laid his head down and, to the rhythm of the waves and the rocking of the boat, he fell asleep. It was the perfect end to a perfect day!

And then, suddenly, the day was not so perfect.

The sky turned black. The lake, too.

And a wild wind stirred the waves up tall and stormy.

The boat rocked right. The boat rocked left. The boat rocked up and down. The boat rocked so hard, in fact, that Jesus' friends were sure they would all drown.

But Jesus slept right through it – except for the odd snuffle and snore.

'Jesus!' his friends called at last. 'Jesus! Wake up! We're all going to drown!'

So Jesus woke up. Then he sat up. Then he rubbed his eyes and he stood up. It was all anybody else could do to stay on their feet. But Jesus stood up! And then, very calmly, he said to the wind, 'Quiet now.' And he said to the waves, 'Settle down.'

And they did!

Then Jesus turned to his friends and said, 'You didn't need to be frightened. You didn't have to worry. All you had to do was trust me. See, everything is calm.'

And so it was. The sky was blue. The lake, too. And the little waves splashed happily at the side of the boat.

It was a perfect day, again!

From *The Lion Storyteller Bible*, text copyright © 1995 Bob Hartman

Aunt Mabel's Table

Here's one of my all-time favourite stories. Try telling it using the character descriptions that I have suggested. (See page 40.)

There were five cans on Aunt Mabel's table.
One for Aunt Mabel.
One for my oldest cousin Sue.
One for my Uncle Joe.
One for my older cousin Tom.
And one for me, Alexander.
There were five cans on Aunt Mabel's table. And not one of them had a label.
'I got them on sale at the supermarket!' beamed my Aunt Mabel.
'This is like a game we play,' whispered my cousin Sue.
'You have to eat whatever is in your can,' sighed my Uncle Joe.
'I got dog food, last time!' said my cousin Tom.
I want to go home, I thought. And then I remembered what my mother said. 'Your Aunt Mabel is different from other people. Just try to be polite.'
There were five cans on Aunt Mabel's table. So my Aunt Mabel picked up the biggest one.
She looked at its top. She looked at its bottom. She looked all around its sides. Then she held it to her ear and shook it. Everybody listened.
'Sounds like sweet, juicy peaches,' guessed my Aunt Mabel.
'Sounds like round red tomatoes,' guessed my cousin Sue.
'Sounds like those little white potatoes you always buy!' moaned my Uncle Joe. 'The kind that make me sneeze!'
'Sounds like dog food,' guessed my cousin Tom.
'I don't know,' I said. 'It just sounds all splashy and splooshy to me.'

My Aunt Mabel marched the can to the counter. She fished a can opener out of a crowded drawer. And in a flash, she cranked off the lid.

'Look!' she cried. 'Look! It's peaches! I love peaches! Who's next?'

There were four cans on Aunt Mabel's table. So my oldest cousin Sue picked up the smallest can.

She looked at its top. She looked at its bottom. She looked all around its sides. Then she held it to her head and shook it. Everybody listened.

'Sounds like soft flaky tuna,' guessed my Aunt Mabel.

'Sounds like thick pink salmon,' hoped my cousin Sue.

'Sounds like that lumpy meat spread you always buy!' moaned my Uncle Joe. 'The kind that makes me burp!'

'Sounds like dog food,' guessed my cousin Tom.

'I don't know,' I said. 'It just sounds all soft and mushy to me.'

My cousin Sue took the can to the counter, and she carefully opened it. But when she turned around with the can between her hands, there was this disgusted look on her face.

'Spinach,' she groaned. 'I hate spinach! Who's next?'

There were three cans on Aunt Mabel's table. And they were all about the same size now. So my Uncle Joe sighed and picked up the one in the middle.

He looked at its top. He looked at its bottom. He looked all around its sides. Then he held it to his ear and shook it. Everybody listened.

'Sounds like pears in thick syrup,' guessed my Aunt Mabel.

'Sounds like tinned sweetcorn,' guessed my cousin Sue.

'Sounds like those kidney beans you always buy!' moaned my Uncle Joe. 'The kind that make me itch!'

'Sounds like dog food,' guessed my cousin Tom.

'I don't know,' I said. 'Sounds like... sounds like... sounds like... peas.' I was trying to be polite.

My Uncle Joe took the can to the counter and he opened it.

But when he turned around with the can between his hands, there was an even more disgusted look on his face.

94

'Kidney beans!' he moaned. 'I'm itching already! Who's next?'

There were two cans on Aunt Mabel's table. So my older cousin Tom picked up the one without the dent.

He looked at its top. He looked at its bottom. He looked all around its sides. Then he held it to his ear and shook it. Everybody listened.

'Sounds like baked beans,' guessed my Aunt Mabel.

'Sounds like mushy peas,' guessed my cousin Sue.

'Sounds like that condensed soup you always buy!' moaned my Uncle Joe. 'The kind you have to add water to.'

'Don't let it be dog food!' cried my cousin Tom.

'Sounds like spaghetti,' I guessed. I was definitely catching on!

My cousin Tom took the can to the counter and opened it. But before he could turn around, I stuck my head over his shoulder and peeked.

'Look!' I shouted. 'I was right! It's spaghetti!'

'I hate spaghetti!' said my cousin Tom. 'I hate spaghetti even worse than dog food! Who's next?'

There was one can left on Aunt Mabel's table. And if I was going to be polite, I would have to eat whatever was in it.

I looked at its top. I looked at its bottom. I looked all around its dented sides. Then I held it to my ear and shook it. It made no sound at all!

For the first time, my Aunt Mabel looked serious. 'It could very well be dog food,' she guessed.

'Or cat food,' guessed my cousin Sue.

'Or beef and liver flavour,' guessed my Uncle Joe. 'The kind that smells so bad.'

'Woof!' barked my cousin Tom.

But I said nothing.

I picked up the can and marched it to the counter. I stuck the sharp end of the can opener into the top. I turned the handle ten times. Then I carefully pulled back the lid.

What I saw was brown. And thick. And gooey.

It was a whole can of...

... CHOCOLATE PUDDING!!

There were five of us sitting at Aunt Mabel's table. Aunt Mabel stuck a spoon into her bowl of peaches.

'Thank you for coming to dinner!' she said to me.

My cousin Sue looked at her plate of spinach and gagged.

My Uncle Joe looked at his kidney beans and started scratching.

My cousin Tom asked to go to the bathroom.

But I remembered what my mother told me.

'Thank you for having me,' I said. Then I stuck a spoon into my bowl of chocolate pudding and – very politely – ate it all up.

Tortoise Brings Food

Here's a good story for practising voices. See what you can come up with for the lion, the hare, the elephant, the tortoise, and the old man. And why not encourage the crowd to do some of those voices along with you! (See page 44.)

The sun was hot. The earth was dry. There had been no rain for many months. And now there was no food. The animals were very hungry.

Lion, king of all the beasts, called his thin and tired friends together under the shade of a tall, gnarled tree.

'The legends say this is a magic tree,' he roared, 'which will give us all the food we need – if only we can say its secret name. But there is only one person who knows that name – the old man who lives at the top of the mountain.'

'Then we must go to him,' trumpeted Elephant, 'as quickly as we can! Before we all starve to death.'

'I'll go,' said the Tortoise, slowly. And everyone just stopped and stared.

'Don't be silly,' roared Lion. 'It would take you for ever! No, we shall send Hare to find the name of the tree. He will be back in no time.'

Hare hurried up the side of the mountain, his long ears blown back against the side of his head. He leaped. He scampered. He raced. And soon he was face to face with the old man.

'Please tell me the name of the magic tree,' he begged. 'The animals are very hungry.'

The old man looked. The old man listened. And then the old man said one word and one word only: 'Uwungelema.'

'Thank you,' panted Hare. And then he hurried back down the mountainside.

He leaped. He scampered. He raced. All the while repeating to himself the name of the magic tree: 'Uwungelema, Uwungelema, Uwungelema.'

But, just as he reached the bottom of the mountain, Hare hurried – CRASH! – right into the side of a huge anthill, and knocked himself silly.

So silly, in fact, that by the time he had staggered back to all the other animals, he had completely forgotten the name of the magic tree!

'We must send someone else,' roared Lion. 'Someone who will not forget.'

'I'll go,' said Tortoise again.

And this time, the other animals laughed.

'We'll have starved to death by the time you get back,' chuckled Lion. 'No, we shall send Elephant.'

Elephant hurried up the side of the mountain, his long trunk swaying back and forth. He tramped. He trundled. He tromped. And soon he was face to face with the old man.

'Please tell me the name of the magic tree,' he begged. 'The animals are very hungry.'

The old man looked puzzled. 'I have already told Hare,' he said. 'But I suppose I can tell you, too.' And then he said that word: 'Uwungelema.'

'Thank you,' panted Elephant. And then he hurried back down the mountainside.

He tramped. He trundled. He tromped. All the while repeating to himself that secret name: 'Uwungelema, Uwungelema, Uwungelema.' But, just like Hare, he was in such a hurry that he failed to notice the anthill. And he too stumbled – CRASH! – right into its side, knocking himself so silly that he, too, forgot the secret name.

'This is ridiculous!' roared Lion. 'Is there no one who can remember a simple name?'

'I can,' said Tortoise, quietly.

And the other animals just shook their heads.

'Enough!' roared Lion. 'It looks as if I shall have to do this myself.'

So Lion hurried up the hill and talked to the old man. But on the way back he, too, stumbled into the anthill and staggered back to the others, having forgotten the name completely.

'What shall we do now?' moaned Giraffe.

'I will go,' said Tortoise, determined to help. And before anyone could say anything, he started up the mountain.

He did not hurry, for that is not the tortoise way. Instead, he toddled. He trudged. He took one small step at a time. And, finally, he reached the old man.

'Please tell me the name of the magic tree,' he said slowly, 'for my friends are very hungry.'

The old man looked angrily at Tortoise. 'I have already given the name to Hare, to Elephant and to Lion. I will say it one more time. But if you cannot remember it, I will not say it again!'

And then he spoke the word: 'Uwungelema.'

'Thank you,' said Tortoise, as politely as he could. 'I promise you that I will not forget.'

And he started back down the mountain.

He toddled. He trudged. He took one small step at a time, all the while slowly repeating, 'Uwungelema, Uwungelema, Uwungelema.'

And when he came to the anthill, he simply wandered round it. For he was in no hurry. No hurry at all.

When he returned, the animals huddled round him.

'Do you know the name?' they asked. 'Did you remember it?'

'Of course,' Tortoise smiled. 'It's not hard at all.' Then he looked at the magic tree and said the word: 'Uwungelema.'

Immediately, sweet, ripe fruit burst out from the magic tree's branches and fell to the ground before the hungry animals. They hollered. They cheered. They ate till they were full – that day and the next and all through the terrible famine.

And, when the famine was over, they made Tortoise their new king. And they never laughed at him again.

From *The Lion Storyteller Bedtime Book*, text copyright © 1998 Bob Hartman

The Big, Soft, Fluffy Bed

This story is a good example of the way that repetition and participation sometimes work hand in hand (see page 47). With most participation stories, you have to explain to the group what they are supposed to do. But in this story, the repetition makes that so clear that I rarely have to ask them to get involved at all – they just join in! This is particularly true of smaller children who can't help squeaking and crying and miaowing along with me after the second or third time.

Granny put Danny to bed – in her big, soft, fluffy bed.

But when she closed the door behind her – closed it ever so slowly and ever so gently – the hinge on the door went Squeeeek!

And Danny woke up with a cry!

'Oh dear,' said Granny, 'I know what we'll do. We'll let the kitten sleep with you, just this once. And she can keep you company!'

So Granny put Danny to bed again – in her big, soft, fluffy bed. With the kitten curled up at his feet.

But when she closed the door – closed it ever so slowly and ever so gently – the hinge on the door went Squeeeek!

Danny woke up with a cry!

And the kitten jumped up with a 'Miaow!'

'Oh dear,' said Granny, 'I know what we'll do. We'll let the dog sleep with you, just this once. He can keep you company!'

So Granny put Danny to bed again – in her big, soft, fluffy bed. With the kitten curled up at his feet.

And the dog stretched out beside him. But when she closed the door – closed it ever so slowly and ever so gently – the hinge on the door went Squeeeek!

Danny woke up with a cry!

The kitten jumped up with a 'Miaow!'

And the dog leaped up with a 'Woof!'

'Oh dear,' said Granny, 'I know what we'll do. We'll let the pig sleep with you, just this once. She can keep you company!'

So Granny put Danny to bed again – in her big, soft, fluffy bed.

With the kitten curled up at his feet.

And the dog stretched out beside him.

And the pig right next to his pillow.

But when she closed the door – closed it ever so slowly and ever so gently – the hinge of the door went Squeeeek!

Danny woke up with a cry!

The kitten jumped up with a 'Miaow!'

The dog leaped up with a 'Woof!'

And the pig rolled over with an 'Oink!'

'Oh dear,' said Granny, 'I know what we'll do. We'll let the pony sleep with you, just this once, and he can keep you company!'

So Granny put Danny to bed again – in her big, soft, fluffy bed.

With the kitten curled up at his feet.

And the dog stretched out beside him.

And the pig right next to his pillow.

And the pony squeezed between them all!

But when she closed the door – closed it ever so slowly and ever so gently – the hinge on the door went Squeeeek!

Danny woke up with a cry!

The kitten jumped up with a 'Miaow!'

The dog leaped up with a 'Woof!'

The pig rolled over with an 'Oink!'

The pony bounced up and down with a 'Neigh!'

And the big, soft, fluffy bed fell down with a crash!

'Oh dear,' said Granny, 'this will never do!'

So she shooed the kitten back into the kitchen.

Walked the dog out into the yard.

Persuaded the pig to go back to her pigsty.

And led the pony into the barn.

Then Granny mended the big, soft, fluffy bed.

She looked at the door.

She looked at the rusty hinge.

And then she went out to the shed and came back with a little can of oil.

Granny squirted the oil on the hinge, then one last time, she put Danny to bed – in the big, soft, fluffy bed.

And when she closed the door – closed it ever so slowly and ever so gently – the hinge on the door... made no sound at all!

And Danny fell fast asleep.

The Clever Baker

Here's a good participation story that I have used in schools for years. Have all the boys beat the batter – Clackety, clackety, clack! Have all the girls play the cat – Yow! Yow! Yow! Have all the female teachers play the dog – Woof! Woof! Woof! And if you're lucky enough to have a male teacher in room, let him play the baby – Wah! Wah! Wah! (Just pick someone else – or do it yourself – if you don't!) Tell them their lines at the start, and then just let the noise build and build! (See page 50.)

Annie was a baker – the best in all Scotland. Shortbreads and buns and cakes – she made them all. And they were so delicious that no one ever left a crumb behind, on table or plate or floor.

Now this was fine for everyone but the fairies, who depended on those crumbs, and who had never had so much as a tiny taste of one of Annie's famous cakes. So one bright morning, the fairy king decided to do something about that. He hid himself among the wild flowers by the side of the road, and when Annie passed on her way to market, he sprinkled fairy dust in her eyes to make her fall fast asleep.

When Annie awoke, she was no longer on the road, but deep in fairyland, face to face with the fairy king.

'Annie!' the king commanded. 'Everyone has tasted your wonderful cakes. Everyone, but us! So from now on, you will stay here in fairyland and bake for us every day.'

Oh dear, thought Annie. But she didn't show that she was worried, or even scared, for she was a clever woman. No, she set her mind, at once, to making a plan for her escape.

'Very well,' she said. 'But if I am to bake you a cake, I will need ingredients – flour and milk, eggs and sugar and butter.'

'Fetch them at once!' commanded the fairy king. So off the fairies flew, to Annie's house. And back they flew, in a flash, with everything she needed.

'Oh dear,' Annie sighed, shaking her head (and still without a plan). 'If I am to bake a cake, I will also need my tools – my pots and pans and pitchers and bowls and spoons.'

'Fetch them quickly!' the fairy king commanded again. But when the fairies returned, they were in such a hurry that they stumbled and sent the pots and pans crashing and clanking across the floor.

'OOH! OWW!' cried the fairy king, jamming his hands against his ears. 'You know very well that I cannot stand loud noises!'

And at that moment, Annie had her plan. She broke the eggs and poured the milk and mixed in the flour and butter. But when she stirred the batter, she made the spoon clatter – Clackety, clackety, clack! – against the side of the bowl.

The fairy king winced at the noise, but Annie could see that it was not loud enough. And so she said, 'Oh dear. I am used to having my little yellow cat beside me when I bake. I cannot make my best cake unless he is here.'

So the fairy king commanded, and the fairies went, and came back at once with the cat.

Annie put the cat under the table and, as she mixed the batter, she trod, ever so gently, on the cat's tail.

And so the spoon went, 'Clackety, clackety, clack!'

And the cat went, 'Yow! Yow! Yow!'

And the fairy king looked even more uncomfortable.

'Oh dear,' said Annie again. 'It's still not right. I'm also used to having my big brown dog beside me when I bake. I don't suppose…?'

'Yes, yes,' sighed the fairy king. 'Anything for a taste of that cake.'

And the fairies were sent for the dog. Annie put him next to the cat, and he soon began to bark.

And so the spoon went, 'Clackety, clackety, clack!'

And the cat went, 'Yow! Yow! Yow!'

And the dog went, 'Woof! Woof! Woof!'

And the fairy king stuck a fairy finger in one ear.

'Just one more thing,' said Annie. 'I am worried about my little baby. And I cannot do my best work when I am worried.'

'All right, all right,' moaned the fairy king. And he sent off his fairies one more time.

The baby was asleep when she arrived, but as soon as she heard all the noise, she awoke with a cry.

And so the spoon went, 'Clackety, clackety, clack!'

And the cat went, 'Yow! Yow! Yow!'

And the dog went, 'Woof! Woof! Woof!'

And the baby went, 'Wah! Wah! Wah!'

And the fairy king put his hands over his ears and shouted, 'Enough! Enough! Enough!'

And everything went quiet.

'Even the best cake in the world is not worth this racket,' he cried. 'Take your baby, woman, and your dog and your cat and your noisy spoon. Go back to your own world, and leave us in peace!'

Annie smiled. 'I'll do better than that,' she said. 'If you promise to leave me be, I'll put a special little cake for you and your people by the fairy mound each day.'

'That's a bargain,' smiled the fairy king, and Annie and all that belonged to her were returned to her kitchen in a flash.

And everyday, from then on, Annie left a little cake by the fairy mound. And the fairy king not only left her alone; each day he left her a little bag of gold, where the cake had been. And they all lived happily ever after.

From *The Lion Storyteller Bedtime Book*, text copyright © 1998 Bob Hartman

David the Giant-Killer

Here's the 'Little – Bigger – Big' retelling of David and Goliath, where I ended up with three Davids instead of one! (See pages 51 and 62.)

Goliath was big.

He had to stoop to get through doorways. His head was always bumping up against the ceiling. And his friends thought twice before inviting him to dinner.

Goliath had a big spear. Ten feet long, at least. With a big iron point. And his big bronze armour weighed a hundred pounds or more.

Goliath had a big voice, too.

And, one day, he used it. He stamped out in front of his army and shouted across the valley to the soldiers camped on the other side.

'I am Goliath!' he bellowed. 'And I dare any of you to come and fight me. Win the fight, and we will be your slaves. Lose, and you must work for us.'

David was little.

Just a boy, really, who looked after the sheep. When he wanted a break from that, he carried cheese to his brothers in the army. And that's what he was doing one day, when he heard Goliath shout.

David was a little angry.

'Who does that giant think he is?' huffed David. Doesn't he know that the Lord God himself watches over us? Why, with God's help, even I could beat that bully.'

So David took a little walk. He went to see the king.

'I want to fight the giant,' he announced.

And the king almost fell off his throne.

'But you are so little,' said the king. 'And he is so big!'

'A lion is big,' answered David. 'And so is a bear. But when they came after my sheep, the Lord God helped me face them and fight them off. He will do the same with this giant.'

'All right,' the king agreed. 'But at least let me lend you my armour.'

The armour was big. Too big. And so heavy that David could hardly move.

So he gave it back. And picked up five little stones instead. And a sling. And his trusty shepherd's staff.

Goliath gave a big laugh when he saw the little shepherd boy.

And he took two big steps.

David ran a little way.

Two more giant steps for Goliath.

And David ran a little further.

They were in the middle of the valley now, and everything was quiet.

Goliath roared a big roar, sucked in a big breath of air, and raised his big spear.

David sneaked his little hand into his little pouch, pulled out a little stone, and slipped it in his sling. Then he spun it round his head and let it fly.

And before the giant could say another word, the stone struck him on the head, and he fell with a big thud to the ground.

David's side shouted a big 'Hooray!'

Goliath's side whispered, 'Uh-oh.'

And from then on, some pretty big things happened to the little shepherd boy. He was given a king's reward. He was promised the hand of the king's daughter. And, one day, he became king himself! The very best king God's people ever had.

From *The Lion Storyteller Bible*, text copyright © 1995 Bob Hartman

Silly Jack

I don't use a lot of props in my storytelling, so this tale is an exception. I gather what I need from the crowd itself (saves a lot of carrying stuff about – and makes the story more personal). I ask for a penny, a cup, a cat (usually a rolled-up jumper), a leg of lamb (shoe with laces) – and then ask a boy to play a donkey and a girl to play the rich man's beautiful daughter. This one has repetition and participation and is one of my favourites. (See page 57.)

On Monday morning, Jack's mother sent him off to work for the carpenter. Jack worked hard, and at the end of the day the carpenter gave him a shiny new penny.

Jack carried the penny home, tossing it in the air as he went. But as he crossed the little bridge over the narrow brook, he dropped the penny and lost it in the water below.

When he told her, Jack's mother shook her head. 'You silly boy,' she sighed, 'you should have put the penny in your pocket. You must remember that tomorrow.'

On Tuesday morning, Jack's mother sent him off to work for the farmer. Jack worked very hard, and at the end of the day the farmer gave him a jug of milk.

Jack remembered his mother's words, and carefully slipped the jug of milk into his big coat pocket. But as he walked home, the milk splashed and splooshed and spilled out of the jug and all over Jack's fine coat.

When he told her, Jack's mother shook her head. 'You silly boy,' she sighed, 'you should have carried the jug on your head. You must remember that tomorrow.'

On Wednesday morning, Jack's mother sent him off to work for the baker. Jack worked very hard, and at the end of the day, the baker gave him a beautiful black cat.

Jack remembered his mother's words, and carefully sat the cat on his head. But on the way home, the cat was frightened, leaped from Jack's head into a nearby tree, and refused to come down.

When he told her, Jack's mother shook her head. 'You silly boy,' she sighed, 'you should have tied a string around the cat's collar and pulled it home behind you. You must remember that tomorrow.'

On Thursday morning, Jack's mother sent him off to work for the butcher. Jack worked very hard, and at the end of the day, the butcher gave him a huge leg of lamb.

Jack remembered his mother's words, tied a string around the meat, and pulled it home behind him. But by the time he got home, the meat was covered with dirt, and good for nothing but to be thrown away.

When he told her, Jack's mother shook her head. 'You silly, silly boy,' she sighed. 'Don't you know you should have carried it home on your shoulder? Promise me you will remember that tomorrow.'

Jack promised, and on Friday morning, his mother sent him off to work for the man who ran the stables. Jack worked very hard, and at the end of the day, the man gave him a donkey!

Jack looked at the donkey. Jack remembered his promise. Then he swallowed hard, picked that donkey up, and hoisted it onto his shoulders!

On the way home, Jack passed by the house of a rich man – a rich man whose beautiful daughter had never laughed in all her life. But when she saw poor, silly Jack giving that donkey a ride, she giggled, she chuckled, then she burst out laughing, right there and then.

The rich man was delighted, and gave Jack his daughter's hand in marriage, and a huge fortune besides.

When he told her, Jack's mother didn't shake her head. No, she hugged him and she kissed him and she shouted, 'Hooray!' And she never ever called him 'silly' again.

From *The Lion Storyteller Bedtime Book*, text copyright © 1998 Bob Hartman

Jonah the Groaner

The story of Jonah – ending and all! You could ask the audience to groan, softly at first and then louder and louder, every time they hear the phrase 'Jonah groaned'. I always do a bit of editing at the end of this story and finish up with one last 'And what did Jonah do? Jonah groaned!' so the listeners can have a really good groan at the end. (See page 62.)

Jonah was a groaner. That's right – a groaner. So when God told him to go to Nineveh and tell the people who lived there to change their evil ways, what did Jonah do?

Jonah groaned.

'Not Nineveh!' he groaned. 'Anywhere but Nineveh. The people who live there are our enemies!'

And when he had stopped groaning, Jonah bought himself a ticket. A ticket for a boat ride. A boat ride that would take him far away from Nineveh.

God listened to Jonah groan. God watched him buy his ticket. But God still wanted Jonah to go to Nineveh.

So when the boat reached the deepest part of the sea, God sent a storm.

'God, help us!' cried a sailor. 'We're sinking!'

'God, save us!' cried another. 'We're tipping over!'

'God must be very angry,' cried the captain, 'with someone here on board.'

And what did Jonah do? Jonah groaned.

'It's me,' Jonah groaned. 'I'm the one God's angry with. He told me to go to Nineveh, and here I am, sailing in the opposite direction. Throw me into the sea and your troubles will be over.'

'God, forgive us!' the sailors cried as they tossed Jonah into the water. And almost at once, the sea grew calm.

'Oh dear,' Jonah groaned, 'I'm sinking.'

'Oh no,' Jonah groaned, 'I'm going to drown.'

'Oh my,' Jonah groaned, 'that's the biggest fish I've ever seen!'

And before he could groan another groan, the fish opened its mouth and swallowed Jonah up!

It was God who sent the fish – to rescue Jonah, and to give him time to think. He had plenty to groan about, of course – the fish's slimy stomach, the seaweed, the smell. But Jonah was still alive – and that was something to cheer about! So Jonah stopped his groaning and prayed a prayer:

'I was sinking, Lord. I was drowning. But you saved me. So now I will do whatever you want.'

Three days later, the fish spat Jonah up on a beach. And Jonah kept his promise – he went straight to Nineveh and told the people that God wanted them to change their evil ways.

'Forty days is all you've got,' he warned them. 'And if you haven't changed by then, God will destroy your city.'

The people of Nineveh listened. The people of Nineveh wept. Then the people of Nineveh changed! From the king right down to the poorest slave, they decided to do what was right.

And what did Jonah do? Jonah groaned. He sat himself down in the shadow of a tree, and he groaned.

'I knew this would happen,' he groaned. 'You are a loving God who loves to forgive. But I still don't like the people of Nineveh and I wish they had been destroyed.'

Jonah fell asleep, groaning. And during the night, God sent a worm to kill the tree. When Jonah awoke, he groaned more than ever.

'The tree is dead!' he groaned. 'And now I have no shade.'

'Oh, Jonah,' God sighed. 'You cry about this tree, but you care nothing for the people of Nineveh. I want you to love them like I do.'

'And finally,' God added, 'I want you to stop your groaning!'

From *The Lion Storyteller Bible*, text copyright © 1995 Bob Hartman

The Fall of Jericho

A simple retelling using a simple 'hook' (see page 62). This is another good story for a large crowd. Divide the audience into three groups: one on the left (the people of Jericho), one on the right (the Israelites), and one in the middle (the wall!), facing the Israelite group. The 'wall' should link arms or do anything to make it more wall-like! as you tell the story, encourage the groups to act out their parts as they come. (And don't give away the line about the wall being thick too soon.)

The walls of Jericho went round and round. Round and round the whole city. The walls were tall. The walls were thick. How would God's people ever get in?

Joshua's thoughts went round and round. Round and round inside his head. He was the leader of God's people now that Moses was dead. But how could he lead them into Jericho?

The sword of the Lord swung round and round. Round and round the angel's head. 'God will lead you into Jericho,' said the angel to Joshua. 'He has a secret plan. All you have to do is trust him.'

The soldiers of Israel gathered round and round. Round and round their leader, Joshua. He told them the angel's plan. He didn't leave out one bit. The soldiers were amazed.

So the army of Israel marched round and round. Round and round the walls of Jericho. Once round each day. Six days in a row. And the people of Jericho laughed.

'Why are they marching round and round? Round and round the walls of Jericho? Is this a parade? Is it some kind of trick? They'll never beat us this way!'

But when the army marched round and round, round and round on the seventh day – they marched round once, they marched round twice. They marched round Jericho seven times. Then they raised their voices. They blew their trumpets. And the walls came crashing down!

The people of Israel danced round and round. Round and round the ruins of Jericho. 'God is our helper!' they sang and they shouted. 'He will never let us down!'

From *The Lion Storyteller Bible*, text copyright © 1995 Bob Hartman

Down Through the Roof

Here's one way of dealing with a story that has a couple of central problems. (See page 63.)

Anna stuck a finger through the hole in her skirt.

How did that get there? she wondered.

She would have run to her mother to have it mended, but her mother was on the other side of the house. And the house was full.

Packed full.

Jammed full.

Chock-a-block full.

Why? Because Jesus was visiting.

The old man and woman standing in front of Anna shifted, and she squeezed into the hole between them. She could see better now.

Jesus was a lot like her father. They both taught people about God. They both prayed beautiful prayers. But Jesus could do something else. Something her father had never done. Jesus could make sick people well! No wonder the whole town had crowded into her house.

Suddenly something dropped on Anna's head.

Anna looked up. And there was another hole – a hole in the roof!

Anna stepped back.

The hole got bigger.

The crowd stepped back.

And the hole got bigger still.

'What's going on up there?' shouted Anna's father. And, instead of an answer, a man dropped through the hole. A man lying on a mat with a rope at each corner. A poor, sick man who could not even move. His friends lowered him carefully to the floor, and Jesus gently laid a hand on his head.

'My friend,' Jesus said, 'the wrong things you have done are now forgiven.'

'Wait a minute!' growled Anna's father. 'Wait just a minute. Only God can take away someone's sins. Just who do you think you are?'

Oh dear, thought Anna. Her father often got angry when he talked with people about God.

But Jesus wasn't angry at all. 'Which is easier?' he said calmly. 'To forgive a lame man's sins, or to make him walk?'

It was all Anna could do not to giggle. What a silly question, she thought. One is just as hard as the other.

'Well,' Jesus continued. 'To show you that God has given me the power to fix what is wrong in this man's heart, I shall fix what is wrong with his legs.'

'Stand up!' Jesus ordered the man. 'You can do it.'

And the man did!

What is more, he rolled up the mat, slung it over his shoulder and walked out through the front door.

His friends climbed down from the roof to join him. The crowd followed behind, cheering. But all Anna could do was stare up through that hole and smile!

From *The Lion Storyteller Bible*, text copyright © 1995 Bob Hartman

The Avenger's Tale

Gaps in the story? Sanctified imagination? Here's the story where I probably broke my own rules. (But I still like it anyway!) (See page 65.)

Every night it was the same. For eighteen years, the same. Ehud would wake up, suddenly, cold and sweating and afraid. And that face, the face in the dream, would be laughing at him all over again.

Shouting, that's how the dream began.

'The Moabites are coming! They've crossed the river and they're heading towards the village!'

What followed next was a mad, rushing blur – a spinning haze of colour and fear and sound. His father's hand. His sister's screams. His mother's long black hair. Goats and pots and tables, running and flying and falling down.

And then, suddenly, everything would slow down again, to half its normal speed. And that's when the man would appear. The laughing man. The fat man. Eglon, king of Moab.

He would climb down from his horse, every bit of his big body wobbling. And with his soldiers all around, hacking and slicing and killing, he would walk up to Ehud's family, each step beating in time with the little boy's heart.

His father, Gera, would fall to his knees. His mother, as well, with his sister in her arms. And then the big man, laughing still, would raise his sword and plunge it first into his father, and then through his mother and his sister, too.

Finally, the laughing man would raise his bloodied sword and turn to Ehud, five-year-old Ehud. But before the king could strike, there would come a sound, a call, from somewhere off in the distance. The king would turn his head, look away for just a second, and Ehud would start to run – run between the burning buildings, run past his dying neighbours, run until the nightmare was over, run… until he awoke.

Every night, for eighteen years – that's how long the dream had haunted Ehud. But tonight, he promised himself, tonight the dream would come to an end. For today, King Eglon of Moab, the fat man, the laughing man, the man who had murdered Ehud's family, would come to an end, as well.

Ehud thanked God for his family, and particularly for his father, and the gift that his father had passed on to him. It was a gift that not even the Moabites could take away, a gift that made him the perfect candidate for the job he was about to do – the gift of a good left hand.

Most soldiers were right-handed. They wore their swords hanging from the left side of the body and reached across the body to draw them from their sheaths. That was what the enemy looked for, that was what the enemy watched – the right hand. For the slightest twitch, the smallest movement of that hand might signal that a fight was about to begin. So, a left-handed man enjoyed a certain advantage, particularly if his sword was hidden.

Ehud rubbed his eyes, rolled off his sleeping mat and reached for his sword – the special sword that he had designed just for this mission.

It was only eighteen inches long, far too short for battle, but just the right size for strapping to his thigh and hiding under his robes. And it was sharpened on both edges so he could cut in both directions. He'd wipe the smile from the fat man's face, all right – even if he had to slice it off!

He'd waited for this day for eighteen years. And for those same eighteen years, the nation of Israel had been paying tribute to King Eglon. For the invasion which had destroyed Ehud's village had also swept across the land and resulted in Israel's surrender to Moab. And so, every year, great quantities of treasure and produce and livestock had to be delivered to the royal palace and presented to Eglon himself, as a sign of Israel's submission.

Today was the day – Tribute Day. And the man chosen to lead Israel's procession, chosen by God himself to walk right into the presence of the king, was none other than Ehud, the left-handed man, the man with the sword strapped to his thigh, the man who was finally in a position to set both himself and his people free.

Ehud thought he would be nervous, but instead he was overcome with a sense of calm and purpose. He led the procession, according to plan, out of Israel and across the Jordan river, past the stone statues of Gilgal and into the palace of the king.

He had imagined this moment for years – face to face, finally, with the man he hated most in all the world. What will I feel? he had often wondered. Hatred? Disgust? The overwhelming urge to reach out and strike Eglon where he stands? All those feelings, he knew, had to be overcome if the plan was to succeed. He had to be submissive, polite and reverential if he was to win the trust of this tyrant. But when Eglon at last appeared, Ehud was shocked by what he actually felt.

The king was still a big man – now far heavier than Ehud had remembered. So heavy, in fact, that his attendants had to help support his weight as he staggered toward his throne. And as for laughter, there was none at all, not even a chuckle – just a hard and constant wheeze as the man struggled to move.

Pity. That's what Ehud felt. And he couldn't believe it. Pity and the surprising sense that, somehow, he had been robbed. This was not the man he'd dreamed of – the fat man, the laughing man, the nightmare man. No, this was a sad and pathetic man, crippled by excess and by power and unable to raise a sword even if he had wanted to.

Still, Ehud reminded himself, there was the mission – the job he believed God had sent him to do. And pity or not, for the sake of his people, he would do it.

And so he bowed and he scraped and he uttered the obligatory words:

'Noble Potentate, Ruler of all you survey, Great and Mighty One.'

Then he stepped aside as, one by one, the gifts were laid before the king. Eglon, however, hardly paid attention. He nodded, almost imperceptibly, and acknowledged each part of the tribute with the slightest wave of his hand. It looked to Ehud as if he was bored with the whole affair, or just too old and tired to care.

When the formalities had finished, Ehud sent his entourage away, then turned to the king and said, 'I have a secret message for you, Your Majesty.'

For the first time, Eglon looked interested. His dull eyes showed some spark of life as they focused on Ehud.

'Silence!' the king wheezed at his attendants. 'This man has something to tell me.'

Ehud looked around, nervously. 'It's for your ears only,' he whispered. 'Perhaps if we could meet somewhere... alone?'

The king considered this, and then nodded. 'Very well,' he agreed. 'Meet me upstairs, in my roof chamber. It's cooler there, anyway. Oh,' and here he glanced at the sword that hung from Ehud's side, the long sword, the decoy sword, 'you will, of course, leave your weapon outside.'

Ehud smiled and bowed, 'Of course!'

That smile never left Ehud's face – not once, while he waited for the king to be helped up to his chamber. For the plan was working perfectly, as all the spies had said it would.

Eglon loved secrets, they had assured him. Dealing and double-dealing, they explained, was how he had hung onto his throne. And that made this plan all the more sweet. For Ehud's robe concealed a secret that the king would never expect!

Finally, the guards called Ehud up to the roof chamber. They looked at him suspiciously. They took away the sword that hung at his side. Then they sent him in to the king.

Ehud bowed again. And the king waved him forward.

'So who is this message from?' asked Eglon, and the cruelly calculating look in his eyes reminded Ehud, at last, of the man he saw each night in his dreams.

'From one of your commanders?' the king continued. 'Or from one of your spies? Or perhaps the sight of all that treasure has convinced you to speak for yourself – to betray your own people?' And with that, the king began to laugh. A little, choked and wheezing laugh, but it was enough – enough to rekindle Ehud's ebbing wrath, enough to force him to play his secret hand.

'No,' he answered firmly. 'The message is not mine nor my commanders'. The message I have for you is from God himself.' And he reached his left hand under his robe and drew his sword.

Three times – that was how he had always planned it. Once for his father, once for his mother, once for his poor murdered sister. But the first blow was so fierce, that the sword plunged all the way in, swallowed up past its hilt in the fatty folds of Eglon's stomach. And even though Ehud tried to retrieve it, all he got was a fistful of entrails and blood.

Ehud locked the chamber doors to buy himself some time, then he hurried out down the servants' staircase.

A part of him wanted to savour this moment – to stand and gloat over Eglon's bloated corpse. But if he was to avoid a similar fate, he needed to run. And he thanked God for the escape route the spies had plotted out for him.

Down from the roof chamber and along the quiet corridors of the private quarters – that was the plan. And, sure enough, he passed no one but a startled maid. He rehearsed it as he went: one more turn, one more hallway, and he would be out. But as he dashed around the final corner, he stumbled over something and fell in a sprawling heap onto the floor.

It was a boy. A little boy. He's not hurt, thought Ehud with relief.

'Who are you?' the little boy asked, as he picked himself up and flashed a friendly smile.

'I'm... umm... it's not important,' Ehud stammered. 'I have to be going.'

'Well, if you see my grandfather,' the boy said, 'will you tell him I'm looking for him? He said he would tell me a story.'

'Your grandfather?' asked Ehud.

'The king, silly!' the little boy grinned. 'Everybody knows that!'

And Ehud just stood there, frozen.

He could hear the chamber doors crashing down. He could hear the shouts of the attendants, and their cries, 'The king, the king is dead! Someone has murdered the king!'

He had to go. He had so little time. But all he could do was stand there. And look at the boy. And look at his own bloodied hand. And look at the boy again. And watch as the smile evaporated from his innocent five-year-old face.

And then Ehud ran. Ran as he ran in his dream. Out of the palace and past the stone statues to the hills of Seirah. The army of Israel was waiting there – waiting for his return. And as soon as he shouted, 'King Eglon is dead!', the army swooped down to the valley below.

Ten thousand died that day. Moab was defeated. Israel was freed. And Ehud had his revenge, at last. And, after much carousing and shouting and celebrating, he rolled, exhausted, onto his mat, looking forward to his first full night's sleep in eighteen years.

But unlike Ehud's enemies, the dream would not be so easily defeated. For as the night wore on, it returned – more real than ever.

There was the little boy. There was the shouting. There was the slashing and the screaming and the dying... Ehud trembled and shook, just as he had done for eighteen years. But when he looked, at last, into the eyes of the man with the bloodied sword, Ehud awoke with a start. For the man with the sword was left-handed. And the killer's face was his own.

From *Bible Baddies*, text copyright © 1999 Bob Hartman

The Generous Rabbit

Another good 'community-building' story (see page 28). I've taken to asking the children for the animals, lately. I start things off with the rabbit, but they take it from there. We end up with some real geographical anomalies – rabbit, sheep, giraffe, dinosaur – but it's fun!

Rabbit shivered.

Rabbit sneezed.

The snow rose up to Rabbit's nose.

Rabbit rubbed her empty belly. Rabbit was hungry and tired and cold.

Then Rabbit stumbled across two turnips near the trunk of a tall pine tree.

So she hopped for joy, picked up the turnips and carried them all the way home.

Rabbit gobbled up the first turnip. But when she got to the second, she was full.

I bet my friend Donkey could use this turnip, Rabbit thought.

So she hopped all the way to Donkey's house, and, because Donkey was not at home, she left the turnip in Donkey's dish.

Donkey was looking for food as well.

Donkey shivered.

Donkey sneezed.

The snow rose up to Donkey's knees.

Donkey rubbed his empty belly. He was tired and hungry and cold.

Then Donkey spied two potatoes, near a fence in the farmer's field.

So he gave a happy 'hee-haw', picked up the potatoes and carried them home.

Donkey gobbled up both potatoes, and then he noticed that a turnip had mysteriously appeared in his dish.

Now how did that get there? Donkey wondered. And being much too full to eat it, Donkey thought of his friend Sheep.

So Donkey carried the turnip to Sheep's house and, because Sheep was not at home, Donkey left the turnip on Sheep's soft bed of straw.

Sheep was looking for food as well.

Sheep shivered.

Sheep sneezed.

The snow rose up to Sheep's woolly tail.

Sheep rubbed her empty belly. She was tired and hungry and cold.

Then Sheep spotted a cabbage in the shadow of a snow-covered bush.

So she bleated a happy 'Hooray!' and picked up the cabbage and carried it home.

Sheep gobbled up the cabbage. And then she noticed that a turnip had mysteriously appeared on her bed.

Now how did that get there? Sheep wondered. And, being much too full to eat it, she thought of her friend Squirrel.

So Sheep carried the turnip to Squirrel's house. And because Squirrel was not at home, she shoved the turnip into Squirrel's tree-trunk hole.

Squirrel was looking for food as well. (Just like everyone else!)

Squirrel shivered.

Squirrel sneezed.

The snow rose right up to Squirrel's ears.

Squirrel rubbed his empty belly. He was tired and hungry and cold.

And then Squirrel sniffed out a few nuts buried deep in the snowy soil.

Squirrel was so excited that he shook his bushy tail.

Then he carried the nuts back to his house.

When he got there, however, he couldn't get in. Someone had shoved a turnip into his tree-trunk hole!

Now how did that get there? Squirrel wondered. And, as he

gobbled up the nuts, he thought of a friend, a friend who could surely use something to eat.

So he pulled the turnip out of the hole and pushed it through the snow, all the way... to Rabbit's house!

Rabbit was asleep, so Squirrel left the turnip by her side and crept quietly back home.

When Rabbit awoke, she was no longer tired, she was no longer cold. But she was hungry again.

I wish I'd kept that extra turnip, she thought. And when she opened her eyes, there it was, right beside her!

Now how did that get here? Rabbit wondered. Then she gobbled it up until she was full.

From *The Lion Storyteller Book of Animal Tales*, text copyright © 2002 Bob Hartman

A Long Journey

Here's a simple 'counting' retelling of the Christmas story that I've used with our playgroup. The kids love to do the counting (as long as I remember to keep it at their pace), and the repetition helps to move the story along.

One, two, three.

Four, five, six.

Seven, eight and nine.

Mary counted the miles. And the donkey's footsteps. And the number of times the little baby kicked inside her belly.

It was a long trip. And a hot trip. And she prayed that it would soon be over.

One, two, three.

Four, five, six.

Seven, eight and nine.

Mary knew, because she counted, that there were many more miles to go.

When they arrived, at last, in Bethlehem, Mary and Joseph looked for a place to stay.

One, two, three.

Four, five, six.

Seven, eight and nine.

They knocked on door after door. But at every door, the answer was the same. 'We have no room here! Go away!'

Mary began to cry.

'It's the baby!' she wept. 'The baby is coming. And I need somewhere to rest.'

So Joseph looked up and down the street once more.

One, two, three.

Four, five, six.

Seven, eight and nine.

And there, at house number ten, he found a door he had missed!

The door opened. The innkeeper smiled. But when Joseph asked if he had an empty room, the innkeeper sadly shook his head.

'Bethlehem is bursting,' he said with a sigh. 'We have no room at all.'

'But my wife…' Joseph pleaded. 'My wife is about to have a baby.'

'I can see that,' the innkeeper nodded. 'But I'm sorry, there's nothing I can do.' And he started to close the door.

'Please!' Joseph cried.

'Please!' wept Mary as well.

And that's when the door swung open again.

'There is a place,' nodded the innkeeper. 'Back behind the inn. It's nothing fancy, mind you. But it's warm and clean and dry. And you can have your baby safely there.'

So he led them to the stable. And there, among the animals, Mary finally lay down and gave birth to God's own special Son.

From *The Lion Storyteller Christmas Book*, text copyright © 2000 Bob Hartman

Bob Hartman, *Angels, Angels All Around*, Oxford: Lion Hudson, 1993

Bob Hartman, *Bible Baddies*, Oxford: Lion Hudson, 1999

Bob Hartman, *More Bible Baddies*, Oxford: Lion Hudson, 2001

Bob Hartman, *The Lion Storyteller Bedtime Book*, Oxford: Lion Hudson, 1998 (also available as *The Lion Book of World Stories*)

Bob Hartman, *The Lion Storyteller Bible*, Oxford: Lion Hudson, 1995

Bob Hartman, *The Lion Storyteller Book of Animal Tales*, Oxford: Lion Hudson, 2002

Bob Hartman, *The Lion Storyteller Christmas Book*, Oxford: Lion Hudson, 2000

All Lion books are available from your local bookshop, or can be ordered via our website or from Marston Book Services. For a free catalogue, showing the complete list of titles available, please contact:

Customer Services
Marston Book Services
PO Box 269
Abingdon
Oxon
OX14 4YN

Tel: 01235 465500
Fax: 01235 465555

Our website can be found at:
www.lionhudson.com